Jennie Lopez

Intentional
UNICORN

BRING your authentic self to thrive
in life and career

Intentional UNICORN

© Copyright 2022, Jennie Lopez
All rights reserved.

For more information, contact:
Fig Factor Media, LLC | www.figfactormedia.com
Jennie Lopez | www.intentionalunicorn.com

Cover Design by DG Marco Alvarez
Layout by LDG Juan Manuel Serna Rosales
Illustrations by Jennie Lopez

Printed in the United States of America

ISBN: 978-1-733063-59-3
Library of Congress Control Number: 2021919566

DEDICATION

To the love of my life Brad for being my rock and being my biggest supporter. Thank you for believing in me, at times more than I do. To my incredible kids, Izzie and Ethan: You are my WHY! I can't wait to see you grow up and show the world how amazing you are!

ALWAYS BE YOU.

TABLE OF CONTENTS

ACKNOWLEDGMENTS

Living in gratitude is the way to continue to live in an inspired, grateful, and forward-thinking way. I want to take this time to thank my family, mentors, and key inspiring people who made this book a reality.

To my FAMILIA! Papi y Mami—Thank you for the values that you instilled in me. Thank you for allowing me to grow up in a way that connected me to everything that I am passionate about. Your incredible support (long driving hours, homework time, long practice hours, and your presence) allowed me to become the mom and the purposeful multifaceted professional woman that I am today. Cha (my favorite sister—and the only one! jajaja)— Thank you for being an inspiration for love, strength, resilience, and creative mindset. I am more proud of being your sister than you will ever know.

To my MENTORS! I have been blessed with multiple amazing mentors and to each of you: Thank you from the bottom of my heart. A few mentors have been life-changing for me, and I wanted to take the time and say GRACIAS!

- Dr. Nicholas Peppas—My graduate school advisor, whose continued support continues to amaze and inspire me.

- Ellen Tobias—my very first mentor in the corporate world and who also became my first sponsor.
- Charles Herington—influential mentor who helped me realize the value I bring by having so many unique strengths. Your advice inspired that very first seed of INTENTIONAL UNICORN.

Each of you taught me so much! Your unconditional support during very challenging times in my life has been pivotal, and I am forever grateful.

<u>To my BOOK PUBLISHER and inspiration!</u> Jackie Camacho-Ruiz, you are an incredible inspiration for many of us! I have learned a ton from you and your team during this process. Thanks for believing in me. Keep shining bright! Fig Factor Team, thank you for your support—you all rock!

Talking about inspiring people... I want to thank **YOU**, dear reader. Thank you for supporting this journey, and trusting me to inspire you. If there is one thing that I would love for you to take away from this book is to own and lead with your UNIQUE-NESS to continue to amplify the definition of success.

FOREWORD

Robert Rodriguez, Ph.D.
President, DRR Advisors LLC

According to the U.S. Library of Congress, the 1939 movie *The Wizard of Oz* is the most seen film in history. The movie's success is largely due to the compelling story, memorable characters, catchy songs, and iconic images such as the ruby red slippers, flying monkeys, and dancing munchkins.

Those who have seen *The Wizard of Oz* may recall that everything appears in black and white at the beginning of the movie. We see Dorothy and her dog Toto on their farm in Kansas. Suddenly a tornado comes forcing Dorothy and Toto to seek shelter in their farmhouse. The tornado whisks away the farmhouse and eventually drops them off in an unknown land.

What I remember the most is the scene that follows. Dorothy awakens and opens the farmhouse door, and suddenly, magically, the movie goes from black and white into bright, vivid technicolor. The color brings the movie to life. The color allows us to see the beauty and richness of Oz.

This is my favorite scene because the transition from black and white to living color is a metaphor that reflects my own career. When I first joined corporate America, everything seemed black and white to me. Things were clear but not colorful, and I wondered what was missing.

It turns out what was missing is that as a young professional, I wasn't bringing my whole self to work. I wasn't being my true, authentic self. For me, one of the reasons was that I was struggling with my sense of identity. I am Latino, but early in my career, I always felt I needed to downplay my Hispanic identity. Mentors and friends told me to downplay my heritage so that people would think I received special treatment or that I was the token minority at the company.

Fortunately, I eventually realized that my Latino identity was a big part of who I am. I began to see my Hispanic heritage as an asset. My Latinoness was a source of strength. My bi-culturalism and bilingualism were differentiators. Once I completely accepted and embraced who I was, my personal and professional life went from being black and white to being in vivid color.

I began to see things differently. This color helped bring light to things that were formally in the shadows. It gave me a much more textured understanding of, and appreciation for, who I was and what I could contribute. With this new perspective, I gained confidence. I became much more comfortable in my own skin. I started to exude executive presence.

In this book, Jennie Lopez provides readers with strategies to help them see things more colorfully. In reading an early draft of this book, I noticed tips and insights that will help others be their true, authentic selves. Jennie Lopez is helping readers to tap into their uniqueness. She does a masterful job of helping readers unleash and tap into those things that differentiate them from other smart and hardworking people.

I have no doubt that this book will be widely influential as both a guide for individuals in their personal quest to reach their potential and as an outline for how organizations can tap the unprecedented reservoir of talent and determination that exists in the workplace.

My various responsibilities have taken me across our nation to over 200 U.S. cities and 22 different countries. Everywhere I have been, I have met the people who make their countries work. I deeply respect their drive and understand how all those energies come together to move their countries forward.

I can honestly say that in every one of those places, I have met people who are totally capable, equally determined, and admirably hungry to take their places in their nation's economic and social leadership. I have seen their ambition to succeed in their bright eyes; I have seen their desires to help their families and future generations in their earnest faces; and their readiness to work hard, learn, and put in the necessary hours in their fierce expressions. I understand that to unleash their full potential, all people need is the opportunity, some guideposts, some safety rails, and some trodden paths marked by those who have broken the trail before them. That is precisely what is provided in this book.

The future of society will not be determined by people who have climbed the ladder of success and then pulled it up or closed the door behind them. It will not be enhanced by a few stars at the top of the pyramid, enjoying economic comforts and adulation. Rather, a truly prosperous and inclusive global future is in the hands of those who share their knowledge, hold out a lifeline, and broaden the upward steps of the societal pyramid at ever-increasing heights. That is what this book seeks to do. That is what Jennie Lopez is doing.

People who are on their upward climb should study the principles set forth in Intentional Unicorn. Leaders who seek the best for their companies and for society should integrate these principles into their company strategies and management practices. We would all do well to pay heed.

Jennie Lopez has given us an advanced look at how intentional unicorns will help write the next chapter of individual and organizational success. In *The Wizard of Oz*, Dorothy had to tap her ruby red slippers three times to make her wish come true. All you have to do is read this book and apply its strategies in order to help make your dreams come true.

Dr. Robert Rodriguez is the founder and president of DRR Advisors LLC, a diversity consulting firm. He is a philanthropist, entrepreneur, writer, angel investor, art collector, academic scholar, and thought leader. Dr. Rodriguez has written three books, including Latino Talent, Auténtico, *and Employee Resource Group Excellence. He holds a doctorate and has taught courses at many leading universities. Many consider Dr. Rodriguez to be one of the nation's leading experts in the area of diversity, and he is the proud son of Mexican migrant workers.*

INTRODUCTION

IF NOT NOW...WHEN?

Let me take you back with me to a very funny but also foundational experience that I had. Several years ago, I got invited to participate in senior leadership training at the company I was working at. Just imagine that you are in the corner of the room watching this unfold. As I entered the room, I scanned to see if I recognized any of the leaders there, but in reality, I think there were only two other people I knew in a room of about 20 participants. I sat down, eager to learn what they had in store for us. Before the training, they decided to do an ice breaker exercise, and they gave us these instructions:

1. Please pick a piece of paper and some markers.
2. Go back to your seat and think of what would be in your memoir when you pass. (I thought, 'Ok morbid. What an engaging way to start this training!' I hope you can hear my sarcasm.)
3. On the page, please write down the title and a drawing that would represent it.
4. You have 5 minutes!

I immediately thought, 'Wait, what...5 minutes....? Does that include thinking too?' The pressure was on! I sat down with my blank piece of paper and my color markers and went blank—no pun intended. I looked around and could not understand how everyone was so engaged from the get-go, with tons of writing and in full work mode. I stepped back and thought, 'Ok, Jennie, do not overcomplicate this. Let's just have fun.'

If there was some legacy I wanted to leave behind, it was to continue empowering people about being the best version of themselves. I do not know what came to me, but I immediately picked up a marker and started drawing. I drew the silhouette. I'm not Picasso, so this was a very basic silhouette that a kid could have easily done. I divided it in half. One half, I kept it without colors, just the black pen I used. This half was my "corporate professional side." It had my hair straight down. She was wearing eyeglasses, professional work attire, and heels. The other side was equally smiling, but it looked very different. She had a colorful outfit and was striking a dancing pose. This side of me was wearing a fun all-the-way-up ponytail.

I stared at my magnificent piece of art (ha!) and started reflecting on how I never felt like I belonged anywhere. In my chemical engineering professional journey, I was "too bubbly," "too outgoing," "too nice," and "too people-focused." Actually, many times I was told, "You do not look like an engineer." In my dancing/fitness journey, I was the "quiet one," "the workaholic," "the nerdy one," and "this is just her hobby."

I looked back at the drawing and realized that my ponytail looked like a horn. At that exact point, I realized, "UNICORN." That's exactly how I felt during most of both careers. I felt like I was sticking out like a unicorn—and not for the best reasons.

At that time in my career, when I was taking this training, I was truly empowered and determined to lead with my unique self. Leading fearlessly to be the role model I did not have when I started. I looked at the drawing one last time, and I had an immediate smile on my face. Heck Yeah! I am an INTENTIONAL UNICORN!

The five minutes were gone! They instructed us to tape our memoirs to the wall. Everyone giggled at my drawing. As you might imagine, it was extremely different from the rest, in truly unicorn fashion.

I looked around and all my peers had incredible things to say, world problems to solve, and medical needs to uncover. I did giggle at my own kiddo drawing as well; oh well. That was the end of the exercise—or so I thought. I was so wrong!

I showed up again the next day in the corner of the location, but this time we were outside the room close to the executive committee offices. All the chairs were placed in a circle. We all showed up and sat down, waiting to see what they would announce. In the middle of wondering, the instructor showed up and said, "Today, we will start the day with a Show and Tell." I thought, 'Ok...what is happening?' She continued and asked us to go to the room and grab our memoirs, because we all had to present them to a very important guest joining us. My heart was going super-fast, but then I thought, 'Well, it is probably the instructor, and by this time, we all had interacted for a full day and started forming some rapport, so it should be ok.' I was wrong again.

When we came back, a new person was already sitting in the circle—the very important guest. The one and only CEO of the company! As we sat in our corners, my face turned all of the colors of the rainbow, full of all crazy emotions. Everyone here is solving important world problems and finding innovative medical solutions. I HAVE A FUNNY-LOOKING UNICORN SILHOUETTE.

It was too late to make any changes. With a big smile and faking confidence, I went on about my story. I laugh now, but at the time, I was truly thinking in slow motion, 'THIS...IS...THE...END...OF...MY...CAREER!' But you know what? I'm sure he did remember mine, because it was so different. Again, in unicorn fashion.

Little did I know that the awkward moment would translate into so much in my life. About a year later, one of the instructors of that training contacted me. She said that my memoir was the one that resonated the most with her, and she asked me if I wanted to turn that story into a speech and participate in one of the biggest events of the company, which is equivalent to a TED Talk. I was honored, humbled, and nervous. Even though doing such a talk was always something I strived to do one day, I was not prepared for it. However, the opportunity was right there. I thought to myself, 'If not now, when?" With nervous butterflies, I accepted the invitation. I put so much work into it and practiced like a machine. The speech ended up being so motivating and engaging that they used it as the closing keynote!

The feedback I got from that event made me realize that this is a message people needed to hear—the more empowered people we have, the more actions people take. We need to create change together to make this world one that not only accepts but craves the uniqueness of everyone.

From that moment, I took "INTENTIONAL UNICORN" as my personal brand and message. This is why you can find me on every social media channel under @ intentionalunicorn. This personal purpose was the one that drove me to start my own business.

Fast forward to about a year ago, I had a friend who told me, "Your energy reminds me of a friend of mine, you have to meet her." This is how I met my amazing, magical, and incredible book publisher and now friend, Jackie Ruiz.

We hopped on a phone call to get to know each other. I was mesmerized! She is a mom, business owner, bestselling author, international speaker, and pilot! What?! MAGIX!

Towards the end of our get to know each other call, before I was going to hang up, I told her, 'You know what? Our worlds will cross again in the future, because I also have a dream of writing a book in the future.' She did not hang up; instead, she said, "Tell me more! What is the book about?" I do not know what came over me, but I pitched my concept and idea in a matter of seconds.

Please understand that this is something that I did not prepare for. When I said, 'I also have a dream of writing a book in the future,' that was the extent of my thinking about it! She listened to me and said, "Let's do it!" For a split second, I doubted myself, but once again, I thought to myself, 'If not now, when?'

Here I am, so freakishly excited about sharing my journey and all of the lessons attached to it with you. The book does have a framework that parallels my personal journey and includes a ton of learning nuggets. As you read my story, think about you as well; think about the learning and how you can apply it to get this unshakeable confidence towards leading as your own intentional unicorn!

The memoir drawing I showed the CEO... little did I know, the start of my personal mission.

Chapter 1

THE INTENTIONAL UNICORN

"Your New Life Begins Today."

Do you ever feel the need to please others? Think about how you think you need to behave around your kids. Is it different from when you are at work? What about when you are at church? Or what about when you are at an interview? How do you feel about having to change who you are, depending on the situation that you are in?

There's a well-known saying that applies: "When you try to please everyone, you please no one." This is why I started this book by defining what it is to be an intentional unicorn, and why it is so important to integrate this into how you go about your goals. I will walk you through my personal journey that will explain how I developed this framework for you to use and bring out your own intentional unicorn.

Are you ready to begin your journey?

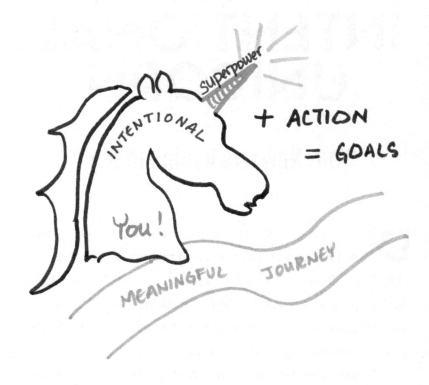

What is an Intentional Unicorn?

WHAT IS AN INTENTIONAL UNICORN?

"Yes, I may still feel like a unicorn, but I am an intentional one."—JENNIE LOPEZ

A unicorn is a mythological creature that has captivated everyone's imagination for over 2,000 years. They were first described as strong creatures, impossible to capture, and with a magical horn with healing powers. With time, the meaning expanded to symbolize freedom, strength, purity, and protection. While there is no hard scientific evidence, some people believe they existed, particularly in China and India.

Whether you believe it or not, everyone agrees in the fantasy that if a horse is going to have a horn on its head, that horn better be special. I know I do! Thus, we see the mystical powers emanating from the single, almost wand-like horn of a unicorn throughout classical literature.

All that to say, you have inner powers, too. When you use them with intention and to point you in the right direction and pursue your passions like the famed unicorn gallops across the prairie, you have brought your inner Intentional Unicorn forward.

People will try to trap her. They will tell you she doesn't exist. They will make fun of her because of not fitting their generic definition of what is acceptable. They will even try to steal her. Even inner fear and doubt will try and sabotage your Intentional Unicorn. But don't let these naysayers get near her. Your Intentional Unicorn is your true authentic self. Your Intentional Unicorn has a beautiful mission in this world.

You may be saying to yourself, "But there is nothing special about me!" To that, I share with you the great news! Everyone came to this world with this magical uniqueness, meant to do incredible, powerful, and meaningful things. Maybe life circumstances have put a shadow on it. Maybe society's rules have put a doubt on it because it does not fit the "norm." I'm putting "norm" in quotations because, in reality... who really defines the NORM? We are missing out on so much from each one of us because of the perception of needing to fit a certain standard.

Now is the time to change this and ensure that each one of us is empowered to let that magical horn shine very bright. It is never late to discover, nurture, empower, and amplify your unicorn and its superpowers.

The time to start was not yesterday because it has already passed. It is not tomorrow because it is not here yet. The absolute best time to start is NOW, and I will be cheering on you along the way during this reading and discovery journey.

We just talked about how the intentional unicorn is your authentic self. Let's go back to that unique horn. That horn has magical powers. I call them superpowers. These are your unique key strengths that set you apart. These superpowers are so strong inside of you that when you use them, you are in flow, on fire, and unstoppable. Why? Because you are using all of your energy towards being in your perfect unique element and not diverting any energy into trying to be someone you are not. You are intentional with your energy instead of wasting it, living your life on autopilot without a purpose.

STRENGTHS VS. SUPERPOWERS

"The things that make us different, those are our superpowers."—LENA WAITHE

Now, don't confuse strengths and superpowers. We may have many strengths that we have developed along the way. But what are those top one or two that set you apart? Those strengths that make you, YOU.

I remember coaching someone; she had to prepare slides before her upcoming interview. One of those slides was about her top strengths. When I reviewed that slide, it had so many bullet points that the font became very small, and I got lost in so many words. The concern about doing this is that you start diluting your value, brand, and message.

After reading her slide, we got into a coaching session. I asked her the following questions: 'Who are you? When you leave that interview, how do you want to be remembered? What do you bring to the table? Why would they be so lucky and fortunate to have you in the organization? What is your true superpower?'

After our chat, she had to do some personal reflection, but she found her genuine answers. Let me tell you that once she drilled that down into her answers—boom!— CLARITY (a best friend to have!) showed up, and she discovered a more genuine, meaningful, and personal 'WHY' for this career move and how she was going to help this amazing organization. And guess what? She got the role, and she is doing amazing. She is leading in a very authentic and powerful way with her unicorn.

Here is another non-work-related example, a silly one now, but not when I lived it. Do you remember the show "So You Think You Can Dance"? One time after work, I heard that they had auditions in Los Angeles, California, that upcoming weekend. Something inside me urged me to buy a ticket immediately and go! I wanted to experience that type of audition.

I got to L.A. the night before and woke up super early to get in line at 5 a.m. I did not expect that people had been camping there since the night before, and my place in line was very, very, very far away from the beginning of it. I was excited, nervous, and confused all at the same time.

By the time I actually got to perform for one minute along with the other nine dancers in my group, it was 7 p.m. I rapidly realized that they were looking for people that could dance all dance genres but excelled at one of them (their superpower). The best hip hop dancers, the best ballet dancers, the best tap dancers, the best salsa dancers, the ones that stood out.

As a dancer, I trained in many genres but did not specialize in any of them. At the end of my minute, I went from 'I think I can dance' to 'maybe not as much as I thought.' Ha!

Even though my un-televised 10-minute short journey did not advance beyond that, I learned a ton from that experience, and I am grateful for it. I learned that knowing your superpower, nurturing it, and developing it brings an additional level of self-confidence that helps you stand out. Also, having the courage to do something outside your comfort zone is always an amazing way to continue learning and growing.

Let's take another example—what is Michael Jordan's superpower? Basketball, of course! Was he a good golfer and baseball player? Yes. Were those his superpowers? No.

Oprah is another amazing example of this. She worked very hard to be a news reporter because she thought that was what success was. She struggled in trying to do something that I'm sure was a strength, but it was not her unique superpower. Once she clicked that her unique superpower was connecting and extrapolating people's stories into priceless nuggets of learning and inspiration, her career flourished, and millions of people have benefited from it.

The learning moment is that whatever that superpower of yours is, you need to be very self-aware of it, nurture it and amplify it. You do this not only for you, but also for all the people you will be impacting along the way.

When we live on autopilot without having the clarity of our unique superpowers, when we do not recognize or empower that unicorn that lives inside of each of us, or when we are not intentional, we simply disappear with the flow. Not having clarity on these elements consume us with worry, stress, fear, comparison, and regret.

Without this horn, the unicorn believes that she is a horse that needs to change, adapt, or play low to fit in or just go with the flow. This life is exhausting and meaningless. It's like going to a restaurant, the server asking you what you want to eat, and responding, 'I don't know, you choose,' and then being upset at what they bring to you.

I lived this life for many years, and I am not saying there were no happy moments, but there was no clear direction, and the worst of it was that I felt trapped without control of my personal or professional journey. This feeling was consuming me. I thought my situation was only work-related. However, it was starting to impact other aspects of my life.

Before continuing to read this book, please do me a favor. Take a deep breath. Actually, scratch that. Shake it off and remove the tension in your body. Sit straight, set back your shoulders, and slowly without tensing your shoulders, ALLOW a deep and slow breath. Do this three times.

How did that feel? Now from a space of focus: Are you ready to take intentional action NOW? If I share with you that it is never late to confidently change the direction of your journey, will you do it? If you do it, who else besides you would benefit from it? How?

DISCOVERING YOUR SUPERPOWERS

"You are stronger than you believe. You have greater powers than you know." —WONDER WOMAN

How can you discover what is inside your horn? How can you enable your superpowers? There are several ways that you can do this. You can start with assessments. There are many assessments out there that can help you point to your top strengths. Just remember that these assessments do not define you; they are just an input of information for consideration and reflection.

There are also easier and faster ways to reflect on this question. You can ask people who know you well (friends, family, boss, peers, etc.) to describe you in three words or share what they consider your top three strengths. You will be surprised at how quickly a few consistent themes start to develop.

I remember texting that question to a few friends, and even though they probably thought that the question came out of nowhere and perhaps found it a little weird, they played along. I even asked my kids, and they both said "caring" at the age of 11 and 8. The same word that friends and peers used.

I never thought of caring as a superpower. The more I reflected on it, the more it made sense because I am a very authentic leader that loves developing, motivating, and inspiring others. Perhaps in the past, I would have been scared of being known for caring because it did not fit the norm of what leadership used to look like. I was afraid that caring was going to be translated as a weakness.

When I started working, caring and leadership were not utilized in the same sentence. However, times have changed, and now more than ever, caring and inclusive leaders are needed everywhere. Now, if people say things like, "You are too nice to be a leader," I reply with, "Being nice is not a weakness; it's a strength in leadership. I care, and that, my friends, is my superpower!" Now that I know this is a superpower of mine, I am proud of this and lead with it!

Another way you can do this is by looking back and connecting the dots. Look back at your personal and professional life and ask yourself: What type of tasks do I usually get asked for help? What type of projects do they typically include me in as a team member or as a leader? You will also see a theme here as you do your personal reflection on your inventory.

I will share an example of mine. For many years, I was offered the leader position in low-performing teams. You know, the teams with the highest rate of HR problems, the ones where they had to let go of the previous leader and they were leader-less for quite a time while they were finding a new one, the teams that were a bit "rebellious" because nobody acknowledged them.

In the beginning, I asked myself, 'Why do they put me in these teams? Why am I being punished?' Then it clicked! Looking back, I realized I had a consistently strong track record of transforming organizations to levels they did not even think possible.

Once you know what these superpowers are and are self-aware of what you have been able to accomplish and what you can deliver, you start driving forward with purpose and intention!

TAKING INTENTIONAL ACTION

"The only impossible journey is the one you never begin."—TONY ROBBINS

The word intention comes from the Latin word *"intentio,"* which means "stretching out, purpose, exertion, effort," and the Old French word *"entencion,"* which means "intent, purpose, aspiration, and will."

"Living With Intention" means living a better-balanced life that is full of meaning and purpose.

I love this quote from Wayne Dyer: "Our intention creates our reality." This is true because the life we live has a lot to do with how we choose to look at and respond to events. It also affects how we interpret what we learn and react to everything in our lives. You either welcome life with a fist or an open hand.

However, something that is missing from Dyer's quote is linking the importance of taking action with that intention. One thing is knowing something, and another is the actions you take with that. They say, "Knowledge is power." I would say, "Knowledge and action lead to power."

Intention without action is just a thought that ends being nothing, zero, nada. Nothing good comes from intention only. Nothing gets created, nothing gets discovered, and nobody benefits from intention only. Think about how many books have not been written, how many goals have not been achieved, how many projects have not been completed or even initiated, and how many meaningful changes have not been in place because they stay in the phase of intention. The key is to take intentional action to drive forward towards your goals.

Sometimes we become paralyzed at the Intention phase because our goals or dreams may seem so huge that we think we need to take this substantial perfect action to make it possible. The key is to break it down into little actions. This way, it is not super overwhelming. Taking action after action helps you keep that momentum that will take you to your goals. Ask yourself: "What is the best next action to take?" One little intentional action after the next turns into progress. Continued progress will turn into the impact that you want to have.

Let's practice! Grab a notebook, a piece of paper, or just open your notes on your phone or laptop. Write a goal that you have wanted to accomplish but have not. Okay, now ask yourself:

- Is my goal measurable?
- How will I know if I achieved my goal?
- When do I want to achieve my goal??
- What steps do I have to take to make it happen?
- What resources do I have to help me through the process?
- How will I make myself accountable in this journey?
- How will I keep track of the progress?
- How will I celebrate the mini wins along the way?

Now break the goal into mini ones and put them in a timeline. How did this exercise help you? What did you learn? Does it feel a bit more achievable?

LET'S TALK ABOUT GOALS

"A goal without a plan is just a wish."
—ANONYMOUS

Is intention the same as goals? No, there are differences between the two of them. A goal is a desired external outcome. Something specific and concrete that you plan to achieve. Goals are focused on the future. The intention is the current intent and purpose. They are in the present, independent of you actually achieving your goal. Your intentions describe how you want to relate to others and how you will drive your actions.

Now, let's explore this concept a bit more with a current example. I have had the goal of writing a book for many years. The goal? A book. I intend to inspire many to be their authentic selves so they can live incredible, meaningful, impactful lives. My intention is reflected in my daily actions, from how I interact with kids, how I make decisions in my job, the material I prepare and share on social media, and how I show up every day.

My intentional action toward my goal was to **DECIDE, COMMIT, and TAKE** the necessary **ACTIONS** to make the book a reality. Did I have everything figured out by the time I decided to start this journey? Of course not! I had no idea how to even start. But little action after little action got me started. I had to LEARN and **ADAPT**.

This was a new journey for me, so I was very intentional in expanding my network and finding the role models and mentors I needed. I had to **INVEST** in myself to continue to grow and have the impact I aspire to have. Last but not least, I now have the honor to **CREATE** and **AMPLIFY** my message by writing this book and **SHOW THE WORLD.**

These intentional actions allow me to share my journey and inspire many of you to discover your superpowers to drive your authentic, meaningful, impactful journey.

Put everything together. All of us are magnificent and unique unicorns. Our unicorns do have a horn with its unique superpowers that are meant to shine bright. Nurture and amplify that superpower to give you the clarity you need to drive your journey. Once you know what your superpowers are, combine them with intention and follow up with action. This is what makes you an INTENTIONAL UNICORN in everything you do, incredibly benefiting all aspects of your life. Being an intentional unicorn will give you the purpose to freely live a very meaningful life.

Last but not least, let's be intentional with the most important superpower that we bring. "What is that?" you may be asking. For many of us, the aspect that we work hard on hiding, changing, or diminishing to fit in, is that amazing superpower that makes us who we are.

This superpower comes from our culture, community, and culture. However, many times it does not fit into the definition of what success looks like. A definition defined by a world that had a much different composition of what the world is today. What brought success to organizations many years ago is not what will bring success now or what will be needed in the future. Now more than ever, we need all to confidently bring our intentional unicorn with clarity and purpose. This, my friend, will free you and enable you to live a meaningful life.

The funny, confident, and bubbly Jennie you see now is the same one that moved to the U.S. back in 2000. However, that Jennie got lost, confused, and swallowed by feedback that made her second guess every move she made.

This, *amigos*, is exactly what we need to STOP. Unicorns are not meant to be diminished and reduced. The biggest lesson I have ever learned was re-discovering who I was. Understanding the power of my unicorn profile and my superpowers gave me clarity on my purpose and the confidence to take action towards doing everything in my power to help others do the same.

All of us are unicorns and are meant to shine bright and make this world a better place. Imagine if all of us UNICORNS know exactly what we each bring and use our superpowers intentionally to not only live impactful and rewarding lives but to create an exciting and limitless world for the ones we love and everyone who will come after us.

Are you ready to unleash your unicorn?

CREATE

ADAPT

TAKE
ACTION

DECIDE

AMPLIFY

COMMIT

INVEST

SHOW
THE
WORLD

How to thrive intentionally!

Chapter 2

DECIDE

"Okay, I'll do both then!"

Do you sometimes stare at your kids, thinking, 'How do they have all this energy?' Actually, let me ask you, do you remember when you were a kid? What were some of the things that you loved to do, and that you could do it all day long if you could?

When we were kids, we had this unstoppable joy and energy. We had a creative, open mind. We craved to learn and love to play with imagination. Have you ever asked yourself, "How did we change?"

I think it was the little moments, the traditions, the joyful moments, and rainbows after the storms (literally and figuratively!) that kept us going with enthusiasm.

Just like a car needs fuel to go from point A to B, we do too! And in this chapter, not only will I share the start of my journey, but I will also share the importance of filling our cups just like when we were kids.

MI CASA, MY CULTURE

"Es que cuando se está lejos es tan dulce recordar, mi corazón se va pa' lla mi Puerto Rico."
—CHARLENE ARIAN

Puerto Rico: la Isla del Encanto. I am from the west of the island, where walking from my house to the coast was a five-minute walk. We had the most beautiful sunsets and starry skies. I still remember going outside to the second-floor marquesina with my dad and sister to see the stars, staring at lightning during thunderstorms, or experiencing the windy calm during the eye of the hurricanes. I know that's an odd thing to do, but we really enjoyed all the little moments, moments like going to the beach or falling asleep in my parent's car after going out for a while on the curvy roads of Puerto Rico. These moments "filled my cup." They nourished me deep inside and gave me joy. They are memories now, and reminders of what filling my cup means.

Now let me bring you back to, hmmm, I was going to share the year but let's keep that a secret (in other words, don't guess my age! Jajajaja <-- Spanish laugh). Let me share my personal journey with you and the importance of our decisions.

My maternal grandparents used to live five houses away. It was like growing up in two houses with a very close family. It was hot and humid to the point that my mom would hop in the car to drive from my house to my grandma's house. Yes, the one that was five houses away!

What made it somehow bearable? Fans and the ocean. My house had a gazillion fans in every corner (it looked like a fan farm ha!), and the nice thing is that you would get a breeze from the coast occasionally.

In the morning, it was rise and shine. The morning alarm clock was usually the neighbor's rooster or dog. Then you would get an afternoon rain. The nights were loud with the sound of *"coqui...COQUI.... COQUI!!!"* (which is a super small frog endemic to Puerto Rico, the size of a one-cent coin but as loud as a power mower or a motorcycle—facts!).

At home, music and humor were front and center. It must have come through all the previous generations. My grandpa used to be a singer in a group—he even had a few recordings. He used to be quite the dancer, singer, and joker. He was the life of the party. I remember him telling us stories from when he was young and used to dance at many local mambo dancing contests.

Growing up, my parents would always play music, and my mom would sing. The weekends were filled with music from Olga Tañón, Juan Luis Guerra, and many more. I believe this is why my sister and I have very strong music and creative genes.

At every birthday "marquesina" party, my dad was

the life of the party, dancing nonstop with everyone. He actually got the nickname of the "Energizer Bunny" because he could not stay still. Now my sister and I can proudly say that we also inherited that gene.

Our family was not that much different from other ones. It is part of our awesome culture. Our culture is filled with history, music, family values, resilience, humor, faith, and pride. We euphorically meet people (even strangers) with a ton of candor, a hug, and a kiss. We celebrate everything. If Miss Universe was from Puerto Rico, the next day there was a huge parade and it was proclaimed an actual holiday on the island—and the same thing would happen if the winner of a big sports event (such as a big boxing match) was Puerto Rican. Similarly, in my household, every single A grade was celebrated!

In our Latinx culture, we put family first; we take care of each other, and ensure that we accomplish huge goals as a team. We are very close as a culture. This does not mean that things were all "perfect full of rainbows and confetti," but our passion for everything we do, combined with our humor, gives us a very unique "resilience" superpower to endure and thrive over everything.

We even have this motto: *"A mal tiempo, buena cara,"* which means that even in the hard times, you keep moving forward with a great outlook on what could happen. The awesome thing is that no matter what, when not-so-good things happen, everyone comes together to work towards whatever goal there is. I mean everyone: family, friends, peers, neighbors, and people that you'd never met before.

This culture was my childhood, upbringing, and the only truth I knew. You can imagine how big of a wake-up call I had later in life, when I realized that it was very different in other places.

YES TO BOTH: ACADEMICS AND ARTS!

"We can't plan life. All we can do is be available for it."
—LAUREN HILL

My parents emphasized the importance of great grades and education at all times. They were very strict with that, expecting only A grades from us. At the same time, they were also very supportive of our passion for the arts.

I started dancing at three years old, taking ballet classes in this small studio, where my mom used to be a fitness step instructor in total '80s fitness gear.

Everything was going well with the exception of the asthma condition that I had developed. It got very burdensome with multiple practices a week were followed by visits to the hospital for breathing treatments. This is why I had to stop taking dance lessons—something I was super passionate about.

My mom learned that swimming was a good sport

for people with asthma, so she enrolled me in swimming classes. Swimming, together with intense medication and treatments, helped me focus on a new sport that eventually took me back to dancing, but this time in the water. Synchronized swimming was my life for many years, from childhood through my early teenage years.

And yes, it is a sport! I learned a ton about dedication, discipline, teamwork, and competition through those years—not to mention all the learning about the multiple ways of how to wash your hair after applying all that crazy, intense gel, so it does not move in air or water. My favorite memories include working towards all the increasing levels of mastery, the summer camps at Puerto Rico's Olympic training facility, and competitions as a solo and with my team.

Unfortunately, the end of my synchronized swimming years was marked by a foot condition that took me out of the water right before a very important competition, "Juegos Centroamericanos y Caribe" (An Olympic-type of sports competition for Central America and the Caribbean), that I had trained for a long time.

My passion for water continued to evolve, and eventually, I became a lifeguard and swimming instructor for kids, which was my very first job at age sixteen. And to this day, I have continued to teach aqua fitness classes. I just love the water! You cannot take the island nature out of this girl.

As a teenager, I also found a passion for singing. I sang in my school's choir for many years, also helping to choreograph our yearly school and hometown music theater performances. I even got to play the lead character in *The Sound of Music.* Yes, imagine the Puerto Rican version of Julie Andrews singing: "The hills are alive...with the sound of music." I truly loved every single minute of it.

In parallel, I managed to focus on my studies and maintained a 4.0. GPA. Math was my favorite subject. At some point, I thought of becoming a math teacher. Two of my grandparents were teachers. The love for teaching that I have always had, started when I was a toddler.

My mom says that she still remembers me fully awake or sleepwalking (I was a bad sleepwalker when I was a kid) teaching the ABCs that were on top of my Strawberry Shortcake kitchen to all of my stuffed animals. She said that I would keep my roster and give them bad grades or get mad at them when they were not behaving.

Now that I think about those days, maybe I was emulating how my parents would get so mad at me because even though I got all As in every subject—I did get all Cs in conduct. I still don't understand; conduct did not count! But I could not stay still; I would talk nonstop in my classes, and play cards in the back of the chemistry class when I was bored and very hyper. When my chemistry teacher would pull me aside, asking me why I would not pay more attention in class, I would say, 'When will I ever use chemistry in real life?' Let's hope she does not read this book and finds out that I ended up studying chemical engineering!

This hyper type of conduct went on for many years. It was not until after I was in high school that we discovered that one of the asthma medications I was taking was very dangerous for kids. This drug made kids hyper-active and made them gain a ton of weight. Who knows what other side effects this drug caused; but it was so bad for kids that it is now banned from the market.

This explains my super hyper days, and why a teacher threatened me once with masking tape telling me that she was ready to tape me down to my seat. Well, that only happened once, because my "mamma bear" came to the rescue, and that was the end of my struggle with my teacher.

FINDING MY FLOW

"Passion is energy. Feel the power that comes from focusing on what excites you." —OPRAH WINFREY

My parents were super dedicated to ending my asthma struggle. We spent several years driving weekly to San Juan (about a three-hour drive each way) to get my injections, and it worked. Once my asthma stabilized, I was able to go back to dancing.

Very quickly, I woke up to the reality check that I had to start again from zero. I was training with very petite, young, super slim ballerinas in my super odd teenage hormone-changing and asthma-medicated inflated body. I felt very out of place in that room.

Every time I went to practice, I looked at the slim, coordinated girls, and then there was me. I just wished so bad to look like them so my teacher would not be so hard on me and my body. I felt that I was embarrassing big time my parents with my plenty to catch up on awkward moves during the recitals.

I made a new friend in the studio that taught me a lot. She was deaf and could not hear the music, but her incredible ability to feel the vibrations from the floor and ballet barre made her succeed at dancing. That taught me so much and brought me so much perspective. Here I am, complaining and feeling so down on myself for something so minor, compared to other people's real challenges.

When you have a gift and passion for something, it comes to you one way or the other. I was able to catch up and fall in love all over again with dancing. I don't even know how to describe it, but I still get teary-eyed when I get to perform, see my kids perform, or simply watch a beautiful dance performance. They are happy tears. When I dance, I get lost, in a great way. It is like nothing else matters, and I just feel joy—I'm in the flow!

MY PROFESSIONAL DANCING YEARS

"Determination, with an optimistic attitude is the key to success."—DALAI LAMA XIV

In high school, I was thinking about what I wanted to be when I grew up; I was thinking of moving to New York to work in Broadway. I had my dreamy plans developed together with a good friend of mine at that time. In our plans, we were moving in together, working as waitresses to pay the bills until we would land our first Broadway role. Lights, camera, action!

That dream was short-lived, because my dad was pretty much like, "Nope, you will become an engineer and go to school here in Mayagüez (my hometown), at el Colegio (hometown University of Puerto Rico campus), and that's it!" I'm sure he used more eloquent words, but that's exactly how I heard it!

At that time, I was very frustrated, but then I thought about it and decided to become a "rebel." Well, this is my very lame version of being a rebel at eighteen years old. I told him that I would become an engineer, but I would be the opposite of him. He is a mechanical engineer, so I decided to become a chemical engineer. (Once again, let's not tell my chemistry teacher!)

At the time, I understood where my dad was coming from and wanted me to go to school to get a stable job and career. At the same time, the thought of not dancing anymore would paralyze me.

I had a choice, but why one and not the other one? I made a decision! (Drum roll, please.) I told my parents, "Well, FINE...then I'll do both," meaning I was going to do my bachelor's in chemical engineering, but I was going to continue to dance and pursue my dreams of becoming a professional dancer. Did I know how? I had no clue—but my determination to do both was louder than anything I had experienced yet, and I knew I would figure it out.

It takes about five years to complete your bachelor's degree in chemical engineering at the University of Puerto Rico, with all of the elective classes and including at least one internship to get the needed experience when you go to the real world.

During that time, I trained and trained in dance. I became a professional dancer. I performed with dance companies. I danced in several marketing campaigns and TV commercials. I also was a dancer at a daily family TV show and got the opportunity to dance and choreograph for special award shows. My favorite part was dancing as a backup dancer for famous Latin singers such as Julio Iglesias, Ednita Nazario, Many Manuel, and others.

I have no words to describe the thrill of being on stage; the lights, the costumes, the art you are creating to entertain others, and the music that takes you away to a happy world. The dancing kept me in flow.

The dance world was fierce, and there was a ton of competition. However, looking back, I don't think I got in my head in any of those auditions where I got the part. I truly enjoyed the moment and got lost in dancing. The times I would doubt or hesitate, that's when they would not go my way. Doubt and comparison can be your worst enemies; I learned that I did my very best when I was only focused on enjoying and learning from the experience.

My college years took a ton of time management and pure dedication. My Monday through Friday looked very similar week after week. I would wake up very early to start with 6:30 a.m. classes back-to-back until about 2 p.m. At that point, I would drive three hours to San Juan to do the TV show ("EL SUPER SHOW"). When the traffic was bad, I changed many times in the car in the middle of a traffic jam. I became a quick-change magician! Looking back now, what in the world was I thinking? Obviously, I do not recommend this—it's not safe. I was at the make-up and hair chair by 5 p.m. to get dressed and head to the studio for show time.

After we did the live show, we would stay for rehearsals. I would often drive somewhere else for other events and rehearsals separate from the show. Then I drove back two and a half hours (less traffic) to get home after midnight, sleep a few hours, and do it all again. Weekends were study time or show time with other dancing engagements. Overall, it was a very busy schedule.

FILLING MY CUP!

"Love what you do, do what you love."—WAYNE DYER

Many people still, to this point, ask me: "How did you manage to do so many jobs?" I realized from my early years in college that I did not see all my work as a dancer as a JOB. Yes, I was getting paid, but for me, it was the thing that was keeping me at flow in every other aspect of my life. It gave me the joy and energy I needed for my studies. It was FILLING MY CUP!

This lesson I use to this date! We are like a cup. Think of your favorite cup of water, tea or *cafecito*. We tend to give, give, give, and do things for others at all times, deprioritizing ourselves. Well, what do you think will happen to your cup? It will pour out every single content until that last drop falls out. Then the cup is empty and dry.

That can happen to you. This is when we can get tired, frustrated, short-fused, exhausted, burned out, and depressed. This is why it is important to fill your cup intentionally! How? Doing things that fill YOUR cup. That can be reading a book, traveling, learning something new, working on cars, exercising, volunteering, photography, etc. There is no limit to what you can do to fill your cup.

When I share this concept, I always hear the same two excuses. The first one: "I am busy, I don't have time." Let's think about that one for a minute. Imagine (I surely hope this does not happen to you), that something bad happens to someone you love. Would you find the time and the way to help them? Of course! No questions asked. Then, why not love yourself the same way you love others?

The second one is: "I do not want to be selfish." A full cup is a happy cup. When you fill your cup, you are at your best. When you are at your best, then you can care and love at your best. So ultimately, it is not a selfish act; it is a selfless act. Happy you, happy life! When you prioritize you, you prioritize everyone you love and care for.

WORKING THROUGH MY INSECURITIES

"If you can dance and be free and not be embarrassed, you can rule the world."—AMY POEHLER

Working on TV was awesome and stressful at the same time. I had already developed some body image struggles when I came back to start training in dance as a teenager, but that was nothing compared to the daily struggle of looking the part when you are on TV. Your job is to look "perfect" all the time. All of us got feedback daily on what needed to be improved or changed.

One summer, I took time off from the show to do an internship in the U.S. for the summer. When I came back, I came back with what I know now is called "College pounds."

I had gained ten to fifteen pounds, and my director said if I did not lose that weight in two weeks, I would be let go from the TV show. It does not help when your family and culture tend to also be a bit too obsessed with weight—and to be completely honest, when you are starting to look *gordita* (chubby) and need to lose weight to be *mas flaquita* (skinny).

I started developing very bad eating habits. Well, let's just say, I stopped eating. My mom would nag me about it. My dad and grandpa kept buying this awesomely fresh-out-of-the-bakery oven bread because they knew how much I loved bread. I got so skinny that you could see my clavicles coming out and my skin, turning a yellowish color. Even then, I remember seeing myself in the mirror as a "big" girl not "fitting the part." My mom was so worried that she took me to the doctor. That was a crazy wakeup call when the doctor said that if I continued this path, I would be anorexic very soon. With the support of my family, I got back to a healthy body and with more confidence and self-love because I needed that to continue to do what I loved to do.

DECISIONS! DECISIONS!

"I don't want other people to decide what I am; I want to decide that for myself."—EMMA WATSON

My senior year in college was a mix of excitement and worry. What is next? I loved the combination of my analytical and artistic careers, and I was not at all ready to give it up.

I went to my very first career fair to get a glimpse of what the real world would look like. I did not prepare at all, because part of me was thinking about grad school anyway. I went to learn from the experience, and yes, I learned.

My very first interview was with the company Colgate. I remember every single question they asked me. I gave them examples of my dancing experiences. The funny thing is that I actually had other jobs. I worked for four years in the lab as a researcher at the University of Puerto Rico, and also had a short internship at another university in the U.S. but for some reason, I gravitated toward giving my dancing career experiences as examples.

I was not surprised when they ended the interview with, "If you love dancing so much, why did you study chemical engineering?" I laugh now, but I remember being so embarrassed. But hey, I learned. For everything I go for now, I prepare to do my best and learn from each experience to do even better the next time.

I prepared for another interview that day, interviewed with Procter and Gamble, and I got an offer! However, I decided to go with my instincts and explore becoming a professor, since I really enjoyed teaching. I realized that the last five years of hard work would be the perfect foundation for grad school.

One decision was done, one more to go: the most difficult one. Do I stay in Puerto Rico, or do I move away?

I come from a small and tight family. Many of my friends have huge families. For me, it was my parents and my younger sister.

I loved my island. At the same time, I was craving independence. I lived with my parents through college, since it was in my hometown. At that time, there was also a big trend of my peers moving to the U.S. in search and hope of better opportunities. I applied to four graduate doctorate programs at top engineering schools in the United States, and got accepted to them all.

I knew this was a hard decision. This was saying goodbye to my family. At that point, I was partially super excited about moving to a new country as an independent adult; an independent woman!

Now reflecting back, what I didn't realize at that time is that I was also saying yes to a significant amount of time without seeing my family, missed birthdays, missed holidays, missed celebrations, raising my kids with "WhatsApp grandparents," seeing my parents grow older from a long distance, and being very far away, feeling helpless whenever the family needs me the most.

With so much excitement and a bright future to come, I had to come up with a decision. This was the moment that I DECIDED to bet on myself and start a new chapter by moving to the United States.

Chapter Key Takeaways

- **The power of DECIDE**—Every decision shapes every chapter of our lives. We can also look at this in a motivational manner. The most amazing experience ahead of you starts with a simple DECISION! When you practice this skill over time, it will increase your confidence. This is also a basic and powerful skill to teach our children and employees. When you decide, you:
    - Start a new chapter
    - Accelerate the goal you are going after
    - Better use your time (your biggest resource in life!)
    - Start to learn and grow (the sooner you start, the sooner you learn and grow!)
    - Help yourself and others focus
    - Build your confidence

Now, bring back your journal and reflect on this question: What is one decision that you have been debating on? Start the journey today and DECIDE!

- **FILL YOUR CUP**—There are so many analogies for self-care out there: putting your oxygen mask first, a multiple-layer wedding cake that crumbles if the foundation is not strong, a phone that slowly breaks, glitches until it stops working. In the end, we are like cars; we need proactive maintenance, fuel, and care to last and enjoy long and fun adventures. My request is for you to please think about what that means for you. How will you intentionally fill your cup? What did you do in your childhood that kept your inner child happy? What is a hobby that you love? Find the time, make it happen! This is just as important as your goals are. Happy and fully charged you = unstoppable you!

Chapter 3

COMMIT

"We are not in Puerto Rico anymore."

Without commitment, nothing happens. What comes to your mind when you hear the word commitment? For example, you may think of an engagement ring, a wedding, or a financial investment in a car or house. In almost every case, there is a long-term implication, and because of it, you have gone through a decision process where your "pros" outweigh your "cons." This is easier said than done. You could get stuck in thinking of everything that could go wrong, and this will stop you from making a commitment that can take you closer to your dreams.

Think of a decision you must make but have not committed yet. Now ask yourself: "Why is this so important for me?" Commitment transforms that promise to yourself into a reality.

In this chapter, I want to share a bit of my story and how I was able to COMMIT and set my journey to great opportunities.

MOVING AWAY

"The secret of change is to focus all your energy, not on fighting the old, but on building the new."—SOCRATES

As I approached the end of my senior year in college, I had four graduate school program offers, a full scholarship and two summer internships with a Fortune 500 company. I was beyond excited with a little hesitation about this new chapter of moving to the United States.

I felt limitless, proud, humbled, and free. As you may recall, I did live with my parents all the way through college, since it was in my hometown. This was the first time I would live by myself as an independent woman.

As I was saying goodbye to my parents and sister at the airport, I felt a mix of emotions. I was happy about my new chapter, but sad thinking it may be long until the next time we would hug again; excited about being independent, but upset and guilty that I felt that I needed to move to another country for what I thought was going to bring me more opportunities. As you can see, a total roller coaster of emotions.

That exact decision had many implications that, at the time, I was not even realizing. Making that decision meant that I was only going to be able to squeeze and hug my family only once a year (if that was even a possibility). It meant that my only sister and I would see each other every few years. This decision meant that I could not be there and help my family when there were moments of need, health concerns, and deaths.

I was saying yes to not celebrating birthdays, holidays, and milestones together as I did when I grew up with them. This decision translated into feeling so helpless and in agony when big earthquakes and hurricanes took place that impacted my family, friends, and island.

Saying yes to this move and eventually staying meant that I was raising kids with "WhatsApp grandparents" and not the very close relationship I had with my grandparents that lived five houses away. This decision meant watching your parents grow old from a distance and constantly regretting not being there with them.

Saying all of this, I am very aware that I am very lucky to have my story when many of my immigrant friends do not get to see their country or family at all due to many more complexities in their journeys. I like to bring this awareness, because many times, we can get so immersed in our own reality and judge others based on our experience when in fact, all of us have our own unique, challenging, and growing journeys.

A beautiful lesson I have learned in my life is "Do not judge someone's inside by their outside." Our unique struggles and journeys build our character; if we are intentional with how we apply the learnings, we can develop incredible superpowers from these experiences.

WE ARE NOT IN PUERTO RICO ANYMORE

"Sometimes you win. Sometimes you learn."
—JOHN MAXWELL

My internship was in Chicago, and my graduate school was in Indiana. I remember driving and getting mesmerized by both cities. I would turn the radio on full volume and would totally feel like Carrie Bradshaw in *Sex and the City*. I am an independent woman! This is my time!

The reality was that I really misjudged how big of a change this was for me. In my mind, I was very focused on being independent. I thought that my experience would give me the confidence I needed to succeed, no questions asked.

Then I got hit with a "boom" and a wake-up call. I realized it was a first in everything: new country, new culture, and new language. In Puerto Rico, we do learn English since Kindergarten, but at least in my case, I never practiced it growing up—and I was not very confident in speaking it fluently.

The culture in Puerto Rico is loud, super friendly, and team-based. In contrast, this culture was much quieter, everyone minding their own business, and with way more social distance than I was used to (and this was when social distance was not a "thing"). Imagine the incredibly scared face of one of my lab partners when I leaned toward him to give him a hug and a kiss when we introduced each other. I am not exaggerating when I say that I still have this memory in slow motion in my head. Me slooowwly leaning towards him and him slooowwly moving and leaning back (imagine the move from *The Matrix*), scared of what was happening at that moment. I am not sure if he felt flattered or terrified, but for sure, this was a miscommunication of cultures.

This was my first time living by myself. I had no personal finance acumen whatsoever. Growing up, I didn't have to worry about house bills, insurance, and medical bills. Now I was making decisions on the little I knew, and realized very quickly that I was making all the wrong moves.

For example, I bought a small used white Pontiac (his name was Casper!) and had no clue that I needed to buy insurance. What was car insurance?

I rented a very small one-bedroom apartment, all excited about it, and quickly realized that after rent and main bills, I had $100 left over for the month for everything else (food included). For a few months, I had a bed as the only piece of furniture in that apartment. Then taxes came in, and I lost it. Taxes?! What is that? I never had to work with that. I did not know that there was no money taken away from my stipend, so I ended up owing a lot of money for taxes and used a credit card to pay it—it was another no-no that I did not know about at that time.

Well, like my favorite singer Alanis Morissette says, "You Live, You Learn." Slowly but surely, I was able to add a small kitchen table for four (this was my office), a small TV, and a futon. Once I had that, then I felt like I was on top of the world again. Celebrating the little wins and mini-moments in life brings you joy, confidence, and a sense of accomplishment—and that's always good.

I DO NOT BELONG HERE

"What sets you apart can sometimes feel like a burden, and it's not. And a lot of the time, it's' what makes you great."—EMMA STONE

I still remember my first day in grad school vividly. I walked into this humongous campus (especially compared to the small buildings at my undergrad college). I walked towards the room where we were going to have our welcome and orientation meeting. Right before I got into the room, the professor who was at the door stopped me and said, "I am sorry but this is only for graduate students," to which I replied, "Yes, I am in the right room." Then he said, "I mean, chemical engineering graduate students," to which I replied again, "Yes, I am in the right room." He seemed confused but welcomed me once I showed my paper with the information.

Quickly scanning the room, I realized this room looked very different from my undergraduate rooms back home, where 70% were females in chemical engineering. When I sat down, I realized there were three females in the group, and I was the only Latino/Latina representation in the entire group.

They kicked off the orientation room with, "Let's go around the room and say your name and the school you come from." I was so relieved, because that was something I could really say in English with no problem. I waited patiently for my turn and very proudly said, "Jennifer Lopez from the University of Puerto Rico!"

As soon as I said that, one of the other students quickly said, "The University of Puerto Rico? Is that even a real university? How did you get here?" Many people laughed, making me feel very uncomfortable and somehow ashamed. I was ashamed because I lost my confidence with that comment, and I did not know how to best respond to him in an articulate way.

Back then, I had to really think about what I was going to say, translate it to English in my mind, and then say it. Instead, I sort of smiled just to "fit in," trying not to bring attention to myself and make that a very uncomfortable situation. I still remember that moment like it was yesterday, and it has been over twenty-two years since that happened.

This transition to graduate school was hard. Not only

did I not feel very welcomed, but also I could not follow the classes very well because of the language and the teaching style of some instructors. Let me explain: back home, chemical engineering came super quick to me. Of course, I studied, but I still had time to dance, hang out with friends, and still had all A's. Here, I found myself completely immersed in studying and at times, back in my apartment, translating some things from the class with a dictionary.

Some classes were easier to follow. Others, even with days and sleepless nights of study, I would get a 12% (yes, you read that right) on an exam. For me, 12% was an extreme failure. That's not an F, that's like a mega F, or an FF! I remember going back super ashamed of my grade, and the professor said that it was a good grade because the average was 9%. WHAT?! 9% was the average? What was I learning from that?

That same professor was biased towards male students. It was very obvious, because we would be walking by each other, and if I was walking with a male graduate student, he would say, "Hello, insert name of the male student here," and not even acknowledge that I was there. This was the same professor who sort of greeted me on the first day of the welcome meeting.

At this point, my confidence dropped to a new low; I did not feel that I belonged in that place. I was alone; I had no idea how in the world I was going to complete the graduate school program. I let those words from that student during my orientation day mess with my mind: *"How did you even get here?"* Was he right? Was I lucky? Was I a diversity card? How did I even get here? How in the world will I be able to navigate this? I should go back home.

LET'S FIGURE OUT A WAY!

"If you really want something, you can figure out how to make it happen."—CHER

Back home, teamwork is everything. We solve problems together, we work together, we learn together, and we succeed together. I was used to always studying in teams. In graduate school, the first couple of months, I had no team. The study groups were affiliated with their ethnicities. There was the Asian study group, the Indian study group, and the male American study group.

Thank goodness I joined the few girls that were in class, and we ended up partnering together. We could not have been any more diverse in terms of where we were from, our life experiences, our personalities, or approaches, but somehow, it worked! It worked because we had a common goal of finding a "tribe" and succeeding together in this program.

I had a choice: figure it out or go back home. However, there was no way I would go back home after everything I did to earn a space in this program. I had to take action: COMMIT!

I prioritized the goal, the outcome—graduating from the program to expand my future opportunities.

I finally met my research professor, which was a pivotal time in the program, because he is one of the most supportive people I have ever encountered here in the U.S. He is why I selected that program. He was (and still is!) one of the top researchers in the world in the area I had done research back when I was an undergraduate student. Working for him was a blessing. Not only was he extremely smart, but he really took care of developing and growing all of us, his research team.

He guided us every step of the way. He engaged us in many opportunities. He always made us feel like FAMILY! For me, that was the most important thing, because of the alignment with my values and culture. He connected me with other Puerto Ricans on campus, current and previous students. I was able to author two big publications under his mentorship. Who would have thought this Puerto Rican lady's research would be highlighted in two big publications?!

I slowly found my confidence. I went back to do something that I really enjoyed, teaching. I became a teaching assistant. I connected very well with my students, teaching undergraduate chemical engineering courses. All those years of teaching my stuffed animals served me well. I even won the teaching assistant of the year award that year.

I started getting out of my shell and meeting new friends. I realized that your network of friends doesn't need to share the same culture. A group of us formed a new multi-cultural team, and we were able to connect and grow together.

Realizing that you don't have to figure things out by yourself is very liberating. There is power in the network and in finding your tribe. When you find a tribe where you can be yourself, one that is empowering and it is built on trust, nothing can stop you. This environment expedites learning and enriches growth. Have you thought of your tribe? Is it an empowering one? Do you have to make some changes? Yes, that happens! You become like the people you surround yourself with. Choose wisely!

FINDING A WAY TO FILL MY CUP

"If you don't find a way to fill your own cup, other people will drain you dry."—OPRAH WINFREY

At this point, one problem was solved: I did not feel alone anymore. However, I also was not my true energetic self. I knew something was missing. I went back to my lesson on filling my cup, and I realized that I was too immersed in my studies and research and missing my dancing and creative side.

I tried to join dancing teams in college, but the time schedule conflicted with my classes and research. I looked for other options. For example, I asked the dancing teams if I could only join for practices when I could make them, but they said no. I also searched for professional dancing companies; the closest ones were in Chicago (two hours away). I decided to take modern dance classes at Hubbard Street Chicago every other weekend. Slowly, I was recovering that side of me.

What finally brought my continuous state of flow was discovering fitness classes! I had never gone to a gym to take group fitness classes before. My only experience with fitness classes was watching my mom teaching her step aerobic classes in the studio, where I took my first ballet classes.

I fell in love with fitness, especially dance fitness classes. I started to go religiously, and week after week, I transitioned from the back row to the mid row to the front row. The instructors took notice, and asked me if I was interested in becoming an instructor as well. I was so excited but also nervous. The thought of being in front of 100 students, teaching them, almost stopped me from taking action. But I thought, 'Hey, you have danced in concerts with way more people than that, you love teaching, you love dancing and fitness... Jennie, you got this! Let's do this.' I did COMMIT!

I became a certified fitness instructor that year, and that gave me energy and purpose. I was helping others transform their fitness and health and was giving them a sense of community. This decision once again helped me with my confidence, continuous flow, energy, and network. Little did I know at that time that committing to becoming a fitness instructor was going to open a brand-new parallel career in fitness, that would allow me to teach in many fitness facilities, meet wonderful students from all ages, specialize my craft in dance fitness, kids fitness and aqua fitness, and even become a master trainer and international presenter for the company Zumba!

AFTER THE STORM, THE REWARD
"Challenges only make you stronger."—JON GORDON

Now, with my network, a tremendous mentor (my research advisor), and a continuous state of flow, I was taking action after action with great momentum. Even though my advisor really wanted me to continue towards my Ph.D., I decided to complete my Master's degree and explore the corporate world.

I still remember when my advisor wrote me a great letter of recommendation in case I ever changed my mind about going for my Ph.D. It is small gestures like that one that are HUGE for us. That gesture of him writing this letter gave me a sense of confidence and appreciation that I did not have for most of my time in graduate school.

His caring attitude went a long way. This same professor somehow continues to keep a pulse on every single one of his students, and we are a huge family! Every time someone achieves a milestone (promotion, degree, award, recognition), he is the first one to congratulate and communicate it to all of us. I do not know how he does it! He is a role model to follow, for sure.

After two years of hard work with graduate courses and research, I completed my Master's degree in Chemical Engineering. My family saw me graduate, which was an incredible achievement. This achievement goes beyond getting a degree but being able to manage through a tough cultural change and growing up as part of this experience.

At times we may look back with *"ay bendito"* or "poor me," but I appreciate chapters like this because they make us stronger. Now, every time I face a new challenge and find myself asking, 'How in the world will I be able to navigate this?' I look back and say, 'Hey, you successfully navigated the graduate school chapter, you can do anything!'

Chapter Key Takeaways:

- **The power of COMMITTING**—Personally committing to something reinforces your decision to go after your goal with confidence. You can lose momentum, focus, or the goal if you do not commit. You can miss out on amazing opportunities and learnings if you do not commit. Remember, the key is to find your WHY.

Let's go back to your personal goal. Why do you have this goal? Why is it important? Why now? What can be possible if you go after it and achieve it? This will help keep you moving forward when things get difficult or you face challenges. Write it down and journal about it.

- **Look back for confidence**—We have all been able to navigate many obstacles. Next time you encounter one, you may stop with fear. You would probably start second-guessing or doubting if you can move forward and tackle it. Look back at your accomplishments and the challenges that you have been able to overcome. What are some of those examples of challenges that you have been able to overcome? Journal about it. How were you able to overcome it? What were the general steps? What were the skills that helped you? What was your guiding force? What resources did you leverage? What was your personal state? Those personal examples will give you the confidence and assurance that you can do it! You can navigate any challenge thrown at you just as you did in the past.

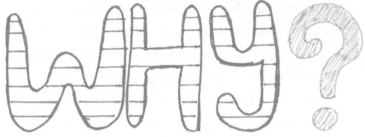

Why do you have this goal?
Why is this goal important?
Why you?
Why now?

Chapter 4

TAKE ACTION

"When there is passion, there is a way."

Imagine you are inside of a movie set, and the director asks everyone to be quiet and says, "Lights, Camera," and that's it. No "Action," no movie! You can have the greatest of intentions of all and decide and commit, but if you do not take action, nothing gets started, created, or grown.

In this chapter, I'll share some examples of how taking action has incredibly changed my life by creating opportunities that I did not think would be possible. I know taking action is not always easy, and we can stay in our heads, thinking about taking action. I also share strategies on how to work through this when it happens.

Think about one thing you have thought about but have not taken action yet. A difficult conversation? A career change? A vacation? A change in your habits? Starting a new project? Whatever that action is, write it down in your journal, and after reading this chapter, try to journal about what you learned here and take that first action you must to make it happen.

Now back to my story....

HERE I COME, CORPORATE WORLD!

"Do one thing every day that scares you."
—ELEANOR ROOSEVELT

Finally, I had made it! I got a full-time job. I had my professional attire, parking lot tag, badge, lab coat with my name on it, steel-toe shoes, hard hat, and safety glasses. I was ready to learn and give the best of myself!

Not long after I started, it felt like a déjà vu of moving to the U.S. for grad school. Once again, I was the only Latina/Latino representation in a group of engineers where most of the team was male. I remember joining the morning meetings and feeling like I had to learn another language. I was totally lost. I joined a new "world" of corporate jargon and English slang, with an insanely high number of acronyms that probably deserved their own dictionary. I would be smiling on the outside, but inside, I was feeling so out of place and asking myself again, 'How will I survive this?'

Many times during that first year, I felt like I did not

belong. One of my first weeks at work, a gentleman saw me and was very surprised. With sort of a smile, he said to me, "Oh wow, you are here?" I quickly responded, very proudly, "Yes, I am!" Then he didn't hesitate and said, "You know we almost did not hire you, because you were way too bubbly for an engineer!" Well, there went my proud moment.

I do not know why he felt the need to share that with me. I did not know how to respond, so I just kind of sort of smiled back and walked away. Little comments like that take away your confidence when you already think you do not belong in that place.

I was the only female on the operations leadership team, and we all sat in a room of cubicles. All the gentlemen met for a long time after our first meeting, talking about the news, politics, and in deep analysis and conversation about sports. I could not relate and had zero interest in those topics. What did I do? I would put my headphones on in my cubicle and work nonstop.

I did not feel included in their men's club, but at that time, that was ok because I thought they were wasting time talking about all of these non-work-related subjects. Instead, I became super focused on my work and was very productive during that time before going and spending time on the manufacturing floor.

However, every story has two sides. I ended up getting feedback that I was acting like I was better than the team and was not a team member. That feedback took me by surprise; I was shocked! I had an initial reaction of taking it personally. I remember thinking, 'It is not me, it is them!' However, I knew that was not getting me anywhere.

When it comes to feedback, one question I always ask myself is, **"What Can I Learn From This?"** In this particular situation, getting defensive would not help anyone moving forward. I realized there was a disconnect between my reality and theirs, and ultimately, I needed to focus on the outcome I was going after. In the end, we all needed to work as a team to deliver on our organization's objectives.

Trying to "fit in" into the men's club and pretending to enjoy the sports and politics discussion was going to be draining and not sustainable. I would have had to learn more about both topics to have a seat at that table.

Instead, I started building trust with each of them, scheduling one-on-one meetings so we could get to know each other better and for me to find commonalities to better connect with them. I also intentionally included in my conversations that I wanted everyone to work better as a team and looked forward to learning from them. I may have also snuck in the fact that sports and politics were not my favorite subjects.

I have learned that the best way to resolve conflict is by taking direct action; otherwise, miscommunication can become a long, toxic situation that harms relationships, teamwork, and business results. This was one of the first work situations that helped me truly listen to feedback and work on it, and I am glad I did because it has helped me realize that every story has different perspectives and points of view.

The goal is listening, understanding, and taking action toward the best outcome for all. Have you ever been in a situation like this? How did you overcome it? What have you learned from it?

I DO NOT FIT IN

"In order to be irreplaceable, one must always be different."—COCO CHANEL

At one of the first trainings our engineering team did, we had to answer a questionnaire where each of us was assigned a color. Based on that color, you were assigned a bit of a personality tendency.

I am no expert on this training, and this is my own quick personal summary of the color meaning: If you were RED, that meant that you were direct and had strong leadership approaches. BLUE was for the ones who were analytical. GREEN was for caring and perhaps introverted in nature. YELLOW was for the social and extroverted ones. The actual training goes into a lot of deep analysis and insights.

Going back to the training, we all took the assessment and were ready for our class. During our class, they gave us our results. Everyone in that room was BLUE except for me, who got all YELLOW. Instead of the team thinking that being different was good, they all looked at me like I was an alien or a unicorn in that room. A peer of mine jokingly said, "Are you sure you are an engineer?" Everyone else started laughing as well. This may have seemed like a small thing, but unfortunately, this was the beginning of a very long and painful journey of people always asking the question, "Is she technical?" and me having to prove myself over and over.

Towards the end of my first year, I was preparing for my first performance review. The review discussion went well, highlighting the results and areas where I was improving. Then I got one single feedback for improvement. "Jennie should dress more like an engineer." What? What did that even mean? Let me share with you that at that time, I was a process engineer in a manufacturing area. I could not even wear a dress, cute heels, or any cute accessories. In my mind, I was already wearing the blandest type of outfits ever: dress pants, button-down shirts, and steel-toe shoes. Add a lab coat, safety glasses, and ear protection to that. What else did I need? Glasses and a calculator in my pocket?

Once again, I tried to do everything I could to fit in. I decided to change my outfit. I eliminated all colors and went with black, white and gray. My goal was to do anything I could to not stand out and blend with others. It got so extreme that my mom once came to visit me at my apartment, and when I was giving her a tour, she looked at my closet and said, *"Nena, parece que vas a ir a un funeral!"* (Girl, it looks like you are going to a funeral!)

I wish more people understood that your leadership style and personality do not have to do anything with your intelligence or technical acumen. The beauty of having diversity with your talent and leaders is that each of them can shine with their unique strengths, qualities, and styles and better connect as a team and the people they serve and help. We need to stop putting labels, visual images, and definitions of what talent and leadership look like because it comes in many wonderful flavors. When leveraged to their unique potential, you get the beauty of true diversity, equity, and inclusion: Magic!

Between not understanding the new lingo and not fitting the standards of what an engineer should look and behave like, I once again felt like I did not belong. I was getting so immersed in my job that I was getting drained. To this, I remembered my lesson of **Filling My Cup.** I was craving my dancing, so I decided to find a dance team and either join them or practice with them.

I didn't know how but I also remember that when I was in college, I didn't know how to do it and figured it out. If I did it once, I knew I could do it again! Remember to **Look Back To Get The Confidence To Move Forward.**

M&MS HELPED ME FIND A NEW WAY!

"There are two mistakes one can make along the road to truth... not going all the way, and not starting."
—BUDDHA

In February of 2003, I told a friend of mine that I was going to look for information on how to try out for the Indiana Pacemates (Cheerleaders for the NBA Basketball team in Indiana). Their auditions were coming up in a few months. I thought that would be logical because I had experience dancing for one of the Puerto Rican basketball teams.

My goal was to experience what a dance audition was like in the United States. This also has helped me when it is time to take action: **Understand the exact goal or outcome** before you decide, commit, and take that key action of yours.

My friend asked me, "why not the Colts Cheerleaders?" Please know that in Puerto Rico, we don't have football. The big sports at that time were basketball and baseball. My only experience with football was attending a game once for a college football team. All I remembered was going to one game in graduate school and screaming "shutdown" very loud instead of "touchdown" (this is how clueless I was about the game).

I also remembered the cheerleaders jumping and

doing a bunch of acrobatic stuff. I told my friend, "Oh no, I don't jump; I dance." He assured me that the NFL Cheerleaders were different, and they did more dancing. Then I got curious and asked him, "When are their auditions?" He said, "Tomorrow!" Wow, that was way too fast. I was not sure if I was ready for it.

Call me crazy or adventurous, but I decided to go. I was leaving my car when I started noticing all these beautiful ladies with big hair, make-up, lashes, and sparkles. I did not know what I was walking into. I was wearing no make-up, black shorts, a black sports bra, black dance shoes, and a ponytail.

I got into the NFL practice field, and there were almost 500 ladies excited and ready to dance. I felt so out of place that I decided to walk back to my car, thinking that "obviously" I was not ready for this type of audition. Getting *closer to my car, I caught myself: Wait, what are you doing? You are here for the experience! Let's go!* I then decided to give it my all and get all the experience in!

I truly had no personal expectations other than learning the dance and performing my best. I just wanted to enjoy the day. To my surprise, the ladies were so nice. I still remember that in one of my leaps, I twisted my ankle, and one of the ladies that was trying out ran to help me, and I was able to dance when it came to my turn in the final audition that first day.

The tryouts lasted almost two months with weekly

cuts. Somehow, I made the first cut! I was thrilled, but in my mind, I thought that making the first cut was the end of my journey when they said there would be a football quiz in a few weeks.

I went back to work on Monday and told my male peers, "You are not going to believe what I did this weekend!" When I shared my adventure with them, they got so excited. They said, "YES! If you make it, do we get tickets?" I smiled and shared, "Nope—this is actually the end for me in this process. There is a football quiz soon, and I have no clue what this game is about." They told me not to worry, and they would work with me—and they did!

They gave me a "Football for Dummies" book, so I could study as a crash course. They also sat with me at the work cafeteria, and with M&Ms, they explained the game. They would say, "This blue one is Peyton Manning." I replied, "Who is Peyton Manning?" and they were shocked! "The quarterback!" I replied, "What's a quarterback?"

At that point, they realized they had to have a serious intervention. They did a great job explaining the game with M&M simulations, and I did my work reading the book, and preparing for the football quiz like it was my professional engineering license.

I passed the football quiz! It was not easy, by the way. Not only did we have to know about the sport but also the players, their positions in the game, and the school they came from. Following the football quiz, it was interview week, in which my engineering and interview skills played well on that one. I also did well during fitness week because of my fitness background. Overall, my dance experience translated very well week after week. After many weeks of hard work, I made it to the final cut!

The final audition was in front of a live audience at the actual football stadium. I was nervous but decided to enjoy every second of it doing what I loved. I was not worried about the competition at this time; in my mind, making it to this final performance was totally unexpected and an incredible experience. To my surprise, I was one of the ladies they announced for the 27 cheerleaders squad of 2003! Me! This Puerto Rican lady who did not know what a quarterback was at the beginning of the process.

I truly enjoyed being part of this organization. The ladies that were part of that team were talented professionals (everyone had to have a full-time job or be a full time student as a requirement), caring, passionate, and great role models. I worked on continuing to learn the sport and continuing to work on my craft—my dancing!

When I joined the team, I did not know how big of a deal it was to be an NFL Cheerleader. I just wanted to join a dance team, but I joined something much more meaningful in terms of the experiences and the leadership lessons.

I had no idea how I would do both my full-time job and this cheerleading job, but I knew I was passionate about it, and **when there is passion, there is always a way.**

I have discovered lately that **it is not about time management but FOCUS MANAGEMENT**. Where your focus goes is where your energy flows, helping you achieve what you are striving for.

The commitment was not small. We had to do multiple appearances per contract, and those were normally late afternoons or long weekends, including the travel. We had practices two to three times a week. Even though we only danced at home games, those days were very long because our call time was six hours before kick off.

I explored my options with pros and cons. The easy option was to say, 'thanks, but no thanks—I do not have time.' Sometimes those easy options feel so comfortable that you tend to gravitate to them immediately, rationalizing all the ways this is a great option. For example, I could have said, 'I have a great job. I should be focused on that,' or 'Jennie, you are an adult now. There is no time for this nonsense,' or 'I have a 24/7 job. What if they call me for work during some practice or game?' Other thoughts included, 'You should be grateful for what you have. Why risk it?' and 'Great, you proved yourself you can do it, now go back to reality.'

However, I knew I had another option: going for it! To make it work, I had to devise a proactive plan to ensure I had a game plan for my what-ifs list. After going over my game plan, the most important thing for me to do was to take action. I needed to take that first step and the first leap of faith into something new. Something scary, fun, and exciting.

How did I make it work? I became very intentional with my time and focus. I leveraged vacation and paid time off when needed—worked with my engineering team to ensure that during my game days, I was not the engineer on rotation covering for emergencies. At every practice and home game, I always studied, worked, or read when I had any downtime. I was the nerdy cheerleader, squeezing work time every minute I could. I made it work! Once again, this filled my cup, and I loved every minute of it.

I loved performing in teams and engaging with people in our appearances, especially with the little girls who saw us as big role models. Talking about appearances, I remember once having an appearance at the company I worked with. Talk about feeling weird wearing a cheerleading outfit in the workplace!

We were signing autographs, and to my surprise, a huge line was waiting for one. All of this was still so new to me. For example, I would have people I work with waiting in line for a long time for my autograph. At the same time, I would be thinking, 'What's so special about my autograph? I sign and approve their qualification packages every week!' I slowly grasped the big chapter I was living, taking every moment to heart. I am forever thankful for this overall experience.

In my second year, I was named captain! I truly enjoyed

working with the squad. I learned how to build teamwork and develop the squad on dancing skills, teamwork, and friendship. I was also selected to be in the Show Team, where we had many shows that included dancing and singing.

One of the most meaningful and eye-opening experiences for me was performing on a Military Tour in Kosovo. This one was several years after the Kosovo War, and we were transported wearing bulletproof protective equipment in tanks just like they were still in war. We delivered basic need items in small villages, and seeing the people run desperately to get a hold of a single item was heartbreaking. This experience started my love for traveling because it made me truly appreciate every little thing we have. Sometimes we get so immersed in our big problems, but in reality, they are nothing to what other people and cultures have to endure.

After my rookie year, I had the blessing of being a captain every single year. I also got to showcase one of my strengths which was choreography, and I got to choreograph sideline routines and several pregame dances! I also got to be one of the two captains that led the team in our big events, such as an exhibition game in Tokyo, Japan, Hall of Fame game in Ohio, and the SUPER BOWL in Miami, Florida. And yes, my friends, I own an XLI SUPER BOWL ring with my name on it! How cool is that? Never in my dreams would I have thought I would experience this journey for six years!

Even with this awesome chapter that lasted six years, I would not share much about it at work. Why? I was scared that people would think less of me because I decided to join the team. Unfortunately, there is a stereotype behind the word "NFL cheerleader," even though none of that was my experience in the real world. We were cheerleaders because of our passion for dancing and helping in the community.

This was a very time-consuming role with little to no pay, so it was not because of the money. The ladies were extremely smart and caring. The friendships last for a lifetime. The other rumor is about wanting to be close to the players. That one I laugh about. We signed two contracts, one for the NFL and the other for the team you work for. We have strict rules where we cannot interact at all with any of the players.

Just to give you an example of how extreme they were with this, they would hire two limos, so I would ride in one and the player in another if we were sent to the same appearance. At the appearance, we would be at two separate tables signing autographs.

Once I accidentally left my cell phone at the practice field. Then later at night, my sister, who lives in Mexico, called my landline and told me that someone with the name of "Mr. Sanders" had my phone that was in the practice field. He called the last number he saw on my phone, which was my sister. I realized after I hung up that it was Bob Sanders, who was a fantastic NFL defensive player for the Indianapolis Colts. Since I was not allowed to talk to the players, I had to go through this whole process of notifying my cheerleader leader, documenting the incident, and having an exchange of five seconds with Bob Sanders outside of my house to get my phone back!

I knew people would talk about me behind my back at work. I actually had a VP at work and several mentors tell me, "Jennie, you know that if you want to be taken seriously here, in management, you need to quit this cheerleading thing." That truly broke my heart, because why would I have to do that? Because of a perception that was not a reality? If only they knew my journey.

This is my plea to everyone reading this book. Please **do not judge a person by their cover.** Instead, use curiosity and learn more about people's journeys. A question I love to ask during interviews or get-to-know-you meetings is: "What is your journey?" Every single time, I learn so much about the person's story, experiences, passions, gifts, and skills!

If we go back to my personal example, I was not "taken seriously" because of the artificial label of being an NFL cheerleader. However, this is what being an NFL cheerleader taught me:

- **LEARNING AGILITY**—I went from not knowing anything about the sport to becoming a veteran captain, spokesperson, and choreographer for the team.

-

- **LEADERSHIP SKILLS**—This leadership role I played for five years.
- **TEAMWORK**—I worked with so many wonderful and diverse ladies and organization leaders.
- **PRESENTATION SKILLS**—I developed this skill when leading workouts, dancing drills, and teaching choreography.
- **SPEAKING SKILLS**—I became the first co-host of the first Spanish TV show, "Cabalgando con los Colts." I also did several Spanish interviews and radio commercials for the organization.

Don't you want these experiences and skills in your organization? We miss this if we stay at the surface when we get to know people. Now I ask you to reflect: How well do you know your peers at work? How well do you know your team? What actions can you take to best know your team so you can continue to build trust and excel together, leveraging everyone's strengths?

Now I am wiser and can better articulate how this experience helped me in my career. If you have a side-gig, hobby, or external experience, make sure you can translate the lessons from that and intentionally use it to amplify other aspects of your life.

I decided to share these highlights with you not to brag but to share what experiences I was able to have by making that single decision of not getting back to my car, committing to the process, and taking ACTION to do my absolute best during the auditioning process.

We often get paralyzed by fear and tend to go back to what is comfortable and known. That comfortable place is stopping you from experiencing greatness and incredible opportunities. Always remember that growth and opportunity take place on the other side of fear. We will talk more about fear in the upcoming chapters.

Chapter Key Takeaways:

- **EXPAND YOUR OPTIONS**—When it comes to decision-making, explore your options. Most people have two options, "do something" or "do nothing." These only two options will drive you crazy and will tend to keep you with a scarcity mindset that may lead to being very anxious about decision-making.

  Instead, make sure you bring at least three options. This will force you to think very creatively and will help you think of other options that you may have not even considered if you had stopped at two. They may not be ideal options, but bring them forward, all of them! Instead of ruling them out in your head, write them down and consider the pros and cons.

  No option is perfect, but considering the pros and cons and evaluating the impact of the options will drive your confidence upwards about your decision-making and will ease the anxiety that may come with the process.

Just as no option is perfect, no situation is permanent. Do not let perfection stop you from moving forward. With any option, there will be learning associated with it and that is the beauty of the journey called progress.

Stopping at one or two options may stop you from experiencing something amazing. If you have trouble coming up with other options, go and reach out to a mentor or a friend. My husband is the best partner I have when it comes to brainstorming options; that is one of his strengths. Find someone (coach, mentor, supervisor, friend, family member) who has your best interest at heart and would enjoy being part of this process with you.

- **Take one step forward BEYOND YOUR COMFORT ZONE**—When you feel like fear is paralyzing you, this is when you need to take the uncomfortable step forward to move away from what is very well known to you. This is where significant growth takes place. The lesson or reward from going beyond your comfort zone is totally worth it.

Take my example from the cheerleading journey. Imagine if I would not have taken that uncomfortable action of going on with the auditions. I would have missed six years of excitement, long-term friendships, leadership lessons, personal development, and meaningful and impactful memories.

Next time you feel that "fear" stopping you.... Stop, smile, and say, "This is great. I'm about to grow! Bring it!"

Now back to that action of yours that you have not taken yet. Journal about the learnings from this chapter. What are your options?

- **TAKE ACTION**—Once you are committed and have explored your options, pick one and take action. Let's not dwell on if it was the "right" one or not because once again, you will stop with indecision taking you back to where you were before.

  If things do not go your way, then think about what you can control and take action. The key is to continue to move forward. Taking action is the only thing that will take you to the results and outcomes you want.

  Here are my top ten reasons why taking action is so important to all of us:

- Leads to your outcomes and results
- Stops you from procrastinating
- Gives you joy and satisfaction
- Takes you to explore and learn new things
- Takes you outside of your comfort zone; therefore, you will experience growth!
- Clears confusion, fear, and doubt
- Opens new doors, maybe ones that you would have never imagined being real for you
- Gets you to quickly learn if you need to adjust, like our "Friends" TV show says, *PIVOT!* (If you don't know what I mean just google it, it's funny)
- Improves your confidence
- Best one: Continuous action becomes a habit. This habit will give you the real definition of joy in life, which is growth.

Decide, commit, and take that next best step... TAKE ACTION!

The benefits of TAKING ACTION

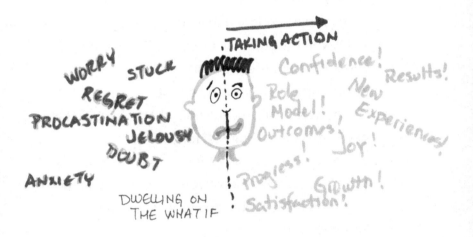

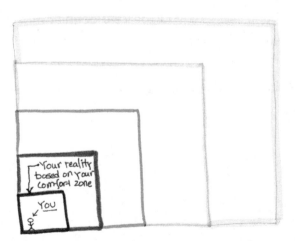

Every time you step forward beyond your comfort zone you amplify your perspective, opportunities and reality!

Chapter 5

ADAPT

"Galloping Against the Current"

In the technology area, there is an expectation of launching a minimal value product, learning, and adapting/improving. There is also a common understanding that the way to improve your product is to "fail fast" so you can learn and improve to get your product much closer to what the customer wants. Imagine if we would still be using the first generation of cell phones. We would have missed the products we have today with their speed, quality, and access to pretty much everything at your fingertips.

Every challenge in life is an opportunity to **ADAPT** and personally upgrade. Let me share a different analogy. Think about this: if you want to gain muscle, what do you do? You go to the gym and work on adding more resistance over time to make that muscle grow. Think about these life challenges as the resistance you are working through to get stronger over time.

Think about a challenge that you had to overcome.

What type of resistance made you stronger? Now, do you want to take this a step further? How can you now leverage that learning to make more impact beyond yourself? Can you teach it? Can you influence or make changes where you work?

In this chapter, I will go over examples of how to ADAPT and WHY we must ADAPT.

PROVING MYSELF!

"Your self-worth is determined by you. You don't have to depend on someone telling you who you are."
—BEYONCE

Once I found my cadence at work and was intentionally filling my cup, I was on a roll. My performance was very strong and I had a great momentum of great performance reviews.

As an early career professional, I would describe myself as a toddler. I just wanted to please everyone. At the same time, I struggled with the feedback I would receive for improvement because it was not about skill or results. I found the feedback that I was receiving to be superficial. However, the feedback was consistent, and I was determined to show them that I could change and become the person they wanted me to become.

Not only did I change the colors of my dress attire

to black, white, and gray, but I was changing many of my natural behaviors. For example, I was holding back in presentations, and acting less bubbly, less energetic. I wore fewer colors and prints, and I was more analytical. I ensured presentations looked like everyone else's—with numbers and a ton of bullet points.

I heard colleagues talking about Harvard Business Review, so I enrolled and learned as well. I started talking with all of the business lingo, even though it did not come naturally to me; but I wanted to fit in.

Another thing that I did which I am not very proud of now, was that I would laugh at jokes on my behalf (on Latino or women stereotypes) just to feel accepted and show that I was a team player. Man, oh man, I know so much better now. However, at that time, I would do anything to fit in and not stand out. I fake laughed at comments like, "Say this again ... it is funny", "Oh, you are on time?", "You should be happy because one of your people just got promoted!"

When I looked everywhere in my company and other companies, I noticed that women and Latinas in high leadership roles were almost nonexistent. My conclusion? In order to have a slim chance of achieving my goal of becoming a leader in the company, I needed to behave like everyone else and work hard for that slim chance that I would one day become a leader too.

One of my biggest challenges was participating in

meetings, especially large meetings or meetings where there was senior management in the audience. English was my second language, and I spent a lot of my time in my head translating and ensuring that I would craft the most perfect, eloquent, corporate-lingo-approved statement.

Just like that was not enough, I also added the pressure of being "perfect" to represent the Latinos. At that time, I was thinking to myself, 'They took a chance on a bubbly Latina to be part of this team, so I will prove to them that they made a great decision.' That, my friends, puts way too much pressure on us.

The problem with waiting for my internal "perfect statement" was that I was missing my timing. By the time I would find the courage to raise my hand to say something (yes, I still do this), someone else would have said it, or the team would have already moved to another topic. Too late!

DO YOU KNOW HOW MUCH SMARTER I SOUND IN SPANISH?

"Do you know what a foreign accent is? It's a sign of bravery." —AMY CHUA

Another thing that I would be extremely embarrassed by was my accent. I am good at reading body language, and I could feel that some people were either thinking less of me or losing their patience with me trying to articulate something. I felt that my accent was interpreted as a lack of intelligence and that killed me for many years.

Many times, friends, peers, and colleagues would say, "Hey, say this word again?" or in front of a group, "Jennie, how do you say this word?" because it would sound funny and make people laugh. At times, I would just get tired of feeling like a monkey in a zoo: "Hey, do this," "do that trick," "good girl." Whenever I would let them know that it was not okay, they would reply with a "Don't be sensitive. It is just a joke."

The sad thing is that I know in their minds, this was a way of making me feel like I was part of the group. But there was a huge lack of personal awareness as to how these actions would truly translate and make me feel.

Do you remember the TV show "Modern Family?" Sofia Vergara (a Colombian actress) played the role of a loud, stereotypical Latina woman. Her name on the TV show was Gloria. My husband and I used to watch every episode and laugh like crazy.

In one episode, the family is making fun of her accent, and she replies, "Do you know how much smarter I sound in Spanish?". Just like any typical joke on the show, my husband started to laugh. My reaction was very different. I have never identified so much with her until that moment. That took my heart and squeezed it. I started getting very teary, and my husband had no idea what was happening. He got worried and asked me, "Are you okay? Did something happen?" and I told him, "You may not understand this, but this is exactly how I feel all the time at work." You won't believe this, but as I am writing this at a Starbucks, I'm getting teary again.

This accent thing was something I was ashamed of. I tried hard to change it, but it didn't go away. I even researched and learned that an accent becomes permanent around age twelve because of how the brain codes language.

At some point, I knew my accent would not truly go away, so instead, I focused on how to gain confidence in speaking. This need for me became obvious when the struggle became real and was impacting my performance.

I remember the panic I would have when giving presentations. I would write word for word everything I was going to say in each slide and rehearse like crazy like I was preparing for a movie scene. The problem with that is that if anyone interrupted me with a question, I would freeze. Literally, FREEZE! That happened many times, and it was the worst feeling.

So instead of using my crutch of "my English is not good," I decided to TAKE ACTION and ADAPT. I explored what options I had to do this. The one I decided to pursue was to join the company Toastmasters club. I truly enjoyed joining that team. My goal was to gain confidence in a second language, and the team was very supportive. Every person in that community was there for many different reasons, and they were very encouraging. Participating in this club gave me the confidence to complete the curriculum and join and win a few competitions.

Let me share an example of how I used the accent learning not only to grow my personal confidence, but also to help others in the company. I was participating in an interview with a colleague. After spending sixty minutes interviewing an individual, my colleague and I had the opportunity to debrief quickly. Almost at the same time, I said, "Wow, he was great!" and he said, "That was terrible!"

As you can imagine, I was quite shocked at how we both interviewed the same exact individual, and came up with such extreme conclusions. I quickly asked him why he thought it was terrible. He said, "Did you hear him? I could not understand most of what he was saying. Speaking like that, he would not have a chance in this company!"

I had to interfere here and tell him I understood everything he said. We focused on the actual content of the interview, his experience, and examples. I also shared how he can be an incredible asset to the team because of his bilingual skills and his experiences in different countries. After the discussion, we aligned on the candidate, moved to the final interview, and shortly after, he got a job offer!

This was a bit early in my career, but an example that reinforced two things. Number one, there is a big bias towards people with accents; some people can disregard a person because of it. Second, representation is crucial in everything. This candidate probably would not have had a chance if it was not because of me having the courage to say something and challenge my colleague.

My lack of confidence because of my accent lasted a very long time. I would be so embarrassed about talking on the phone or ordering at a drive-thru because I would be appalled at the thought of the person on the other side not understanding me and thinking any less of me because of that. You can ask my husband; I often asked him to make calls for me or order for me many times early in our relationship. I still sometimes catch myself saying, "I am sorry, English is my second language," but quickly correct myself and say... English is my second language, my SUPERPOWER.

I now realize that having an accent is the best quality we can have. An accent is not only a sign of bravery, like Amy Chua's quote greatly says, but it is our secret weapon. Having an accent means that we have amazing learning agility and have the incredible power of seeing things through a multi-cultural, multi-experience, multi-dimension lens. Having this amount of knowledge, insight, intelligence, wisdom, and understanding is anyone's competitive advantage. You want this type of superpower on your team! Does your team have this type of competitive insight?

Next time you meet someone with an accent, please

do not stop with the common question asked, "Where are you from?" Instead, be CURIOUS and ask: **"WHAT IS YOUR STORY?"** Curiosity leads to knowledge, power, and understanding. You will be amazed at what you learn from every single individual. I love learning about their resilience, struggles, creativity, wit, perseverance, and ability to push forward and succeed. In return, share yours too. This establishes trust enabling a relationship that is set up to thrive. Let's put to practice what we learned here. Think of an individual on your team (any team) that you want to continue to build trust with. Ask about their story and share yours. Reflect on what you learn.

To wrap this part up, I have an ask to all of us (yes, including myself here): The next time we feel insecure because of our accent, instead of saying, "I'm sorry," let's say, "You are welcome!" Let's own and leverage this superpower of ours!

BE HEARD! INTENT OVER PERFECTION

"When the whole world becomes silent, even one voice becomes powerful."—MALALA YOUSAFZAI

The Toastmasters helped me tremendously in confidence for practiced presentations. However, I was still struggling with the art of speaking on the spot.

Earlier in my career, I was selected to be a Process

Improvement Six Sigma Black Belt. In week one, one of the final exercises was about feedback. The team you have worked with nonstop for a week had to go through this exercise.

In this particular exercise, every person had to be "on the hot seat," and people would go around giving you feedback. The trick here was that you were not allowed to say anything or ask any questions while you were getting the feedback.

All the team members took turns, and then it was mine. Everything was going well until a senior scientist told me, "You need to be very careful about first impressions because you do not look smart. You look like you got an easy two-year degree at best." You can imagine that in that five-minute exercise, all I heard was his feedback. Those words got tattooed on my mind. I still remember that experience like it was yesterday.

There was a reason why I got selected to be in that very highly regarded role, and after spending an entire week learning and problem-solving with the team, that is the feedback that I received! This was one of those instances where I was literally speechless and had no response, even after the entire exercise was complete.

This messed up my confidence once again. Part of me wanted to ignore it, but for every personal thought of "Well, that's just his opinion, ignore it, Jennie," there were a gazillion little voices in my head saying, 'Is this what everyone thinks? What are they thinking of me? I need to be very careful about everything I do and say. I need to prove myself!' This made me pause long and hard before I spoke.

I had a big a-ha moment when I was selected to join an accelerated leadership program shortly after this event. In this leadership program, you were given a very challenging problem to solve for the enterprise. There were no leaders. I worked with another ten talented employees from different sites, and it was our first time working together.

We were assigned to work dedicated to this project for a month. The problem was challenging and not well-defined, and that was on purpose so senior management could assess you. Talking about senior management, some of them would take turns and sit in the room in silence just to watch us and give us feedback (individual and team) every day.

On the first day, I met with one of the senior managers, and he told me, "Jennie, I keep hearing your name and about your great performance; however, I don't see it!" What? I was shocked. My first inner reaction (in my head!) was, 'How dare you judge me. You don't know me." However, I sat down and listened.

He shared with me that he was observing everyone trying to figure out how to organize themselves and tackle the problem while I remained in silence most of the day. He was 100% correct. This was very typical of me. I would always take the time to learn the players. I would stay in silence and assess. In my mind, I would try to do the translations and then try to come up with the perfect opinion or idea in my brain before I said anything, and many times too little, too late after waiting too long. Then at that time, I would raise my hand to say something.

I am actually very thankful for that feedback. I would have shared it differently, but it woke me up. It made me realize that first impressions are very important, and many times you only have a very small amount of time to show your value and help the team. Otherwise, you can become invisible, and we don't want that.

I am not saying to talk just for the sake of talking because nobody likes that. But there are ways to be heard in a way that is authentic to you. Here are a few that I would like to share with you:

- **Share Your Alignment**—Even if you are in agreement, share it. It helps the leader and team with reinforcement and confidence.
- **Speak Up**—If you disagree, let your voice be heard. Think about the impact that being silent can have on someone or the team.
- **Ask Questions, Be Curious**—This can be a clarifying question. Other people often have the same question but are scared of asking. Or it can be a question about what can be possible. This type of question can open brainstorming.

- **Offer advice and ideas**—All ideas are great because they open more options for solutions. Even if the idea is not feasible, it can inspire other creative solutions.

- **Be present and play your part**—Think how the UNIQUE YOU can provide value to the discussion. Based on your unique experiences and knowledge, think about what examples, perspectives, and stories you can share with the team.

- **Do not think about you**—Meaning, do you think how what you are saying is going to be reflected on you? This is probably the one that makes us stop and be quiet. Think of the problem and how your input will help the ones impacted by it. **It is about intent and value, not about you.** You will never be able to control what other people will think or say, but you can control your intent and contribution, and that is far way more rewarding!

When I talk now, I am my genuine self. Yes, you will see bloopers in the videos that I post, and that is perfectly fine. At work, I routinely mess up English slang, like, "We will jump the bridge later instead of crossing the bridge," or "We will talk the walk instead of walking the talk," or confuse the moose and elephant that is either in the room or at the table!

I always ask not to be scripted when I am doing any speaking events. In my personal business, you will see me talking from my heart with my personal, not perfect English, using words that are true to me and no other fancy lingo, not trying to pretend to be someone who I am not.

I am sharing this because now I feel the pressure is off, and the feeling is very liberating! Are people out there making fun of me or the way I talk? Probably! But that's on them, not on me. I cannot control that, and I will not spend energy on that. I can control my ability to say something and how I can add value to everyone I work with.

Now reflect on where in your life you can be more intentional in sharing your voice and being heard. We need your insights, wisdom, and ideas!

IS LEADERSHIP FOR ME?

"Leadership is about making others better as a result of your presence, and making sure that impact lasts in your absence."—SHERYL SANDBERG

Around my fifth year, I was very excited about the idea to become a leader in my organization. I knew that was my desire, my goal, and I knew I could do it. At the same time, I looked around, and there were close to no females in high-level positions.

My goal then became to meet with the very few females out there to learn everything about how they did it, so I could do the same. Most of the female leaders (handful) working in the male-dominated function I was in did not have kids. I knew I wanted to have a family at some point, so I focused on meeting with two females with kids.

The first one told me, "Easy, I outsource everything that needs to do with the kids." I place no judgment here, but I knew that path was not the one I personally wanted. Then I went and met with the other leader. She said, "Well, Jennie, you have to pick; it is either family or work. My daughter is very well aware that mommy has to work and that she will not be able to be at her activities."

Talk about disappointment. I am very thankful for the female leaders that opened the path for us because I know that their situation was different from the options that are starting to open for us now. However, at that point, I was not willing to follow their path and started to think that perhaps leadership and management roles were not for me.

I casually mentioned this conversation to my supervisor at the time, and he stopped me right away and said, "Jennie, you need to look for more perspectives, you would be a great leader, and I want to help you get there." He then connected me with another female that was working in another function. That was one of the best conversations I had. She shared with me that it can be done. She also shared how she prioritized her kids during her career, and she was able to grow on the management ladder.

She said that in the end, it is up to me to set my boundaries. She shared how at the beginning of the school year, she decided what school activities she was going to volunteer for and blocked the time in advance, how she blocked certain lunch days to have lunch with the kids, and how she focused on being present at home while they are awake. These strategies worked very well for me as well!

Another great piece of advice I got was from another female leader, who said, **"Jennie, the company will take what you give to the company."** It was one of those very profound pieces of advice you don't understand right away, but then it becomes crystal clear.

What she meant was that if you give the company 120% and you do it while sacrificing your family time, your quality time with your family, your health, your sanity, your hobbies, your me time, the company will say, "GREAT JOB," and will take it.

In that same way, if you do amazing work for your company, but you do it in a way where you set your boundaries and prioritize what is important to you; if you're creative in how you integrate all the aspects of your life, the company will ALSO SAY "GREAT JOB" and will take that as well.

The moral of this advice is that most times, we can be

our own enemies by putting limits or "rules" on ourselves that are not really there. We may think they are "unspoken, unwritten" rules because that is how "it has been done in the past." But guess what; they did it that way because they may be different from you and me. Different cultures, different family situations, different prioritization, and different times, and it worked for them. That does not mean that this is the ONLY WAY that it can be done.

As a matter of fact, I have seen previous colleagues of mine getting a bit lost or sad post retirement because their entire life was around work. Some have shared that the only thing they regretted was not spending more time with their families.

Another colleague of mine said it well. He was a bit extreme, but he had a point. He shared, "When I die, my graveyard stone will not say BEST SCIENTIST IN THE WORLD; it will say BEST DAD IN THE WORLD."

I'm saying that it is time to break the cycle and start empowering each other to think differently and be creative, so we all can be living at our best in all aspects of our lives.

After I got all of this great advice, I told myself, 'You know what? Let's show them that it can be done. You can be a female, Latina, and a mother, and achieve all your leadership goals.' I took it upon myself to be the role model that I did not have in my function.

Did I have all of the answers at that time? Of course

not! But I knew I was really good at figuring things out, and it became more of a personal mission. My WHY was super strong, and I knew it was going to give me the energy, spark, and perseverance to get to my outcome. Now the next step was how can I ADAPT?

WHO DRIVES MY CAREER? ME!

"There's more to life than being a passenger."
—AMELIA EARHART

I still have a little reminder from a leadership program I was part of. I had a little plaque in the form of a plane that said, "You are the pilot!" I kept it because it is an excellent reminder that at any point of my career, I am the one that needs to take the pilot seat and drive it forward. I can't let anyone else be in charge of my own destination.

During the first five years of my career, I had over ten supervisors. That taught me that sometimes you have amazing supervisors that care about your growth, others that care more about their own growth, and others who, to be honest with you, are just in the wrong role.

Obviously, from all of them, I learned something. I learned what to do and what not to do in the future. I also learned that if I had left my career up to them, I would have still been in my first or second role, re-introducing myself to whoever would be the new supervisor. I also learned the power of having clarity about what you want to achieve and the power of mentorships.

Early in my career, I knew I wanted to grow on the leadership and management ladder. I knew I wanted to be a site head of a manufacturing site and a cross-functional leader. I took it upon myself to write down my career map and drive these discussions with my supervisor. I set them on the calendar and ensured that they were to talk about their careers and no other updates.

Once I became familiar and somehow comfortable in my role, I would have my ears and eyes open to any opportunity I would find that would let me fill the experience gaps I had for my next role or future roles. I asked for projects that were outside of my experience to grow, and also asked for specific mentors to help me learn and grow along the way. This is how I became a project manager for a site-wide project while I was a process engineer; how I led a validation in the science area while I was working as an engineer; and how I led a six-sigma project in the lab while I had no experience with the labs. I always asked for bigger projects, because I knew this was how I was going to accelerate my learning and how I was going to get the experience.

Having that **CLARITY on what I wanted to be helped me grow forward with INTENTION**. Every project I asked for (yes, you heard me right, I asked for them) had a purpose. They would help by adding tools to my toolset, so when the next ideal role would be open, I was more than ready for it. It is like having a clear compass that helps you navigate decision-making.

The decision-making was not only for projects but also for roles. Believe it or not, I said NO to the first promotion to manager opportunity that came my way. It was one of those opportunities where my senior leader said, "Jennie, if you say YES, the role is yours." I went back to my career map and just did not see a clear fit into the puzzle on how that role would help me get to the long-term role of being a site head.

Instead, I waited for that first cross-functional operations manager role that I knew was going to be foundational and key to my long-term goals. While I waited, I continued to be intentional with my experiences. Because of that, when the role that I wanted opened up, even though I was interviewing along another three top performers, I had already accumulated experience doing similar tasks to what I was going to do in this role. Yes, I got it!

Other than clarity, I learned that it is instrumental to know that you do not have to go on this journey alone. This is where MENTORS play a part! They help you learn from their wins and mistakes. They accelerate the path. Even better, great mentors are also your cheerleaders along the way, and believe in you more than you believe in yourself many times.

One of my first mentors was the one that helped me obtain my very first BIG PROMOTION to be a site head of a manufacturing facility. Now I know that she was also my sponsor by that time, and I'll share more about that later in the book.

I met her at a Women in Engineering Network that we had in the company. It was a luncheon, and she and I connected right away. When she left, my friends said to me, "Wow, do you know who you were talking with?" Frankly, I said no; I had no idea. All I knew was that she was very cool and we had a great conversation. She was the only female site head at that time in the U.S. at the company that I was working at.

Later that day, I mentioned that to my supervisor, and he said, "Wow, why don't you ask her to be your mentor?" I had no idea how to even start this conversation, so he helped me contact her. He shared my performance and potential with her, and asked her if she could be my official mentor.

She was one of the best mentors that I have ever had. She also shared with me that she enjoyed our conversations because I always came prepared with updates and questions. Hint: Be prepared for these discussions! Preparation is the key to success.

In the beginning, I was focusing on how to be the best at my role, not really bringing my career into the discussion. She would share stories, ask me great questions (coaching!), and also be a great cheerleader along the way. It was one of those meetings that I would look forward to because I knew I would leave "pumped up" with tons of confidence.

Do you know of the quote "Success is when preparation meets opportunity?" This is exactly what happened when my mentor once called me, now not as a mentor, but as a VP in Manufacturing, and said, "I have an opportunity for you! How do you feel about Kansas City?" The role was to be the site head for the first acquisition of the company. My jaw dropped! I remember telling her, 'Thank you, but I don't think I am ready for such a role.' She said, "I have seen you perform and grow for the past eight years. You are more than ready!"

Listening to those words from her was exactly what I needed. She believed in me, and she said that I was ready; that meant that I WAS READY! And just like that, I accepted my dream role.

Sometimes, we may underestimate the impact we have on someone's life when we play the role of a mentor. Let's continue to be intentional in choosing who are the ones that will play that role for us. Also, be intentional about who and how you will choose to mentor. You do not have to be in leadership to be a mentor. Be the guide and inspiration for someone. Reflect on the people you mentor or can start mentoring. How can you be the best mentor for them? How can you help them transform? How can you change their lives?

Mentorship is a two-way relationship. If I can ask for a special favor, please mentor someone that is different from you. Minority employees are under-mentored because they may not be the first ones to confidently say "pick me," or they may not see themselves in you. Then let's be intentional. This way, both learn from each other and grow together because of it. You, too, can be that person just like my mentor who believes and cheers for someone enough to provide that seed of confidence that many desperately need.

EMBRACING MYSELF!

"I do know one thing about me: I don't measure myself by others' expectations or let others define my worth."
—SONIA SOTOMAYOR

Getting this role was another confirmation that I did have the talent to get to the goals that I had set forth for myself. I also had the realization that when I was trying to please and adjust to what people wanted me to be, or how they wanted me to present, dress, talk, or behave, it was absolutely draining. The heavy feeling and burden you get on your shoulders from the moment you open the door and get into the workplace to start thinking and rethinking every move you make are exhausting.

When you try to please and act, the part people want you to act is not only exhausting but also not sustainable. There are multiple articles out there that go into detail on the amount of emotional exhaustion in actors and actresses. There are two reasons: one is the actual training of resources with the effort, and the second is the continuous tension from emotional dissonance or inconsistency. And for those of us who are not actors, add to that the emotional exhaustion from the actual job that we are to perform. This is not a formula for sustainable growth or success.

Once I clicked on this, I realized that my personal answer was to be the best version of myself and bring the real me to work every day. This was the best compliment to my decision to become the role model I did not have. I took action and adapted, so I could have authenticity as the superpower that would drive my path.

LIFE IS NOT A STRAIGHT LINE

"Life happens. Adapt. Embrace change, and make the most of everything that comes your way."—NICK JONAS

We live in a social media world full of success stories where most people only share their successes. But for every success, there are a ton of adaptations. See, I did not say failures? We may stop trying something we want to do because we think we may fail. Failure is a world that we need to stay away from. Let me be honest with you; that is THE WAY towards growing, experiencing new things, and accomplishing many rewarding goals.

You saw in this chapter the word ADAPT many times. Adapt simply means how we can adjust to new conditions. We have a plan for our lives, and life has a different plan for us. Nobody is perfect; every one of us needs to go out there, try, act and adapt until it takes us to our next destination. I have heard it described like this: "If you want to make God laugh, tell him about your plans." Things will happen in life, but the key is how you react and adapt.

Adapting with purpose will take you to new heights and make your journey a growing one, not one that takes you back in life. When I say adapt with purpose, I mean how you can intentionally learn, tweak, flip, and pivot along with your values to get to your outcome.

Next time you are about to do something new and scary, do not go about it because you think you might fail. Catch yourself with those thoughts and change the vocabulary. Instead, think about how you will take the step, knowing that you will LEARN, and when that happens, it will inform you that it is time to adapt.

Not all the learning has to be painful. Many times, it shows you even more opportunities ahead of time, and you ADAPT to make them a reality. Other times the learnings may be more painful, but those tend to give us the most strength and growth if we learn how to see them as true lessons and find the courage to ADAPT WITH PURPOSE.

One of my favorite stories of adapting with purpose is the one about Walt Disney. When we hear his name, we associate the name with Disneyland and Mickey Mouse—two huge successes! However, if you read his bio, you can learn about his rocky journey full of learnings, and in his case, difficult ones that involved bankruptcy, not having success as an actor, his first famous cartoon being taken away from him, and a mental breakdown.

His story is full of many moments where he had to adapt, but he did it with a purpose. This purpose for him was so big that it took him over 300 rejections to get to the success story that we all now know about. Many people did not believe in Mickey Mouse or later in the park. But he did not give up; he learned each time and adapted. Imagine if, after ten times, Walt Disney would have given up? There would not have been "the happiest place on earth."

Do you remember the TV show Friends? There was an episode where they were trying to get a big couch up a stairwell, and one of the main characters, Ross, kept saying, "Pivot, pivot, pivot," because they had to change their approach quite a bit to be able to get the couch upstairs? If you have not seen the episode, you can google "Friends" and pivot for a few minutes of video and a good laugh.

I once texted the video to my supervisor when I was working on an area of technology. She was just leaving a very tense meeting, and I knew she needed a distraction and a laugh. It was a tense meeting because we were working on an innovative product with tons of unknowns, lessons, and pivots. However, everyone was very connected to the purpose, and it was what helped the team to ADAPT.

Many successful companies are successful because of the ways they ADAPTED. Here are a few examples:

- Nintendo started as a playing card company.
- Airbnb started a housing solution around conferences.
- PayPal started as a mechanism to beam IOUs (signed documents acknowledging debt) from palm pilot to palm pilot (if you even remember them).
- Twitter started as a podcasting platform.
- Netflix's business model was a mail-order DVD service. Do you remember?
- Slack started out of a video game venture called Glitch, and saw a big opportunity out of their communication style.
- IBM. We all remember them as a personal computing giant, and they changed their core business model to IT consulting.

- Play-Doh was first a wall cleaner to take the black residue from coal heaters. Once these types of heaters were not standard, they had to find a new opportunity for their product, and voila! One of our favorite childhood toys emerged!

Some of you may be saying, "Okay, Jennie, that's great for companies or big entrepreneurs, but I'm just a regular person." Well, I hope you know what I'm going to say; you are not JUST A REGULAR person. You are an incredible UNICORN with an endless way of making an impact in your family, community, and world!

See life as a white canvas that you can intentionally continue to write new chapters on. It is a canvas that is not dictated by your past or what people say or believe. It is your own canvas that when you are ready, you can DECIDE, COMMIT, TAKE ACTION, AND ADAPT to live a very meaningful and intentional life.

The best news? You and I have done this. Think about a time of your life when a new opportunity presented itself and you had to change and adapt your way to be able to explore it and make it a reality.

Now think of a time where you had a more painful way of learning, and yet you turned it around. Maybe at the time it was taking place it did not feel good at all, but now you look back and are thankful for that lesson and what emerged from it.

Perhaps you are exactly at one of these places right now and are a bit stuck because of the "What if I fail?" or "I'm a failure." Let's take that word out of our vocabulary. You are about to learn something very valuable in this new chapter of yours, or you already learned a lesson and it is time to ADAPT! You got it, take your purpose to heart and your WHY, and make it happen!

Chapter Key Takeaways:

- **ADAPTABILITY**—Makes you more open to new ideas and gives you the opportunity to grow. Adaptable people are not scared of change, and they make out of every challenge something more meaningful for themselves and people around them. Remember that the only thing that is guaranteed is CHANGE, so we might as well work out our adaptability muscle to be ready for it!

Being adaptable means that you have a growth mindset. Having a growth mindset is essential for you to tackle any challenge that comes your way.

What does it mean to have a growth mindset?

Here are a few examples:

- You are always wanting to learn something new.
- You focus on the process of achieving the goal, not just on the outcome.

- You want to continue to grow and improve.
- You accept the learnings and grow from them.
- You get inspired by the achievements of others.
- You bet on yourself: "I am capable of achieving ....", "I can learn to ....", etc.
- You are comfortable with ambiguity.
- You take ownership.
- You are open-minded.

This is something that you can continue to learn and get better at. Think of an area of your life where you can benefit from having more of a growth mindset. What actions can you take to continue to improve your growth mindset? Is there an area where you need to change course or ADAPT? How?

- **NOT FAILURES ONLY LESSONS**—Asking better questions will help you ADAPT and navigate the lessons and the opportunities ahead of you. Here are a few to get you started:
- What can I learn from this? How can I leverage this learning?
- What other creative options do I have? How else can I pivot from here?
- What resources do I already have to help me think through this?
- What resources can I find to help me navigate through this?

- What is my ultimate purpose or outcome? Is this taking me closer to it?
- Is this enhancing other areas of my life?
- Is this bringing me joy?
- How can I make it enjoyable and rewarding?
- How can I amplify the good?
- How can I mitigate the risks?
- What if it works?

Chapter 6

INVEST

Scary Way of Learning

Have you ever felt stuck with a project or a goal because you don't know the best next step or how to proceed with the next best step? In this chapter, I will talk about the importance of being resourceful and the importance of Investing.

NEW CHAPTER!

"If you can't fly, then run. If you can't run, then walk. If you can't walk, then crawl, but by all means, keep moving."—MARTIN LUTHER KING, JR.

"What about Kansas City?" were the words from my VP when she offered me the role of my dreams at that time. I will be honest with you, when I first heard Kansas City, I thought of Dorothy from the Wizard of Oz and tornadoes.

To my surprise, the city and downtown were just awesome. The best part was that my job was literally six minutes away from our house. Here, I was ready to start the role of my dreams, a brand-new chapter.

Moving to Kansas City meant a lot of newness in our lives. We moved to a new state with a newborn. It meant no friends for a while, because it was not until the kids got to a stage that they were in school or activities that we would start meeting other parents.

We also decided that my husband would stay at home with our kid while I was working. That meant we went from having two nice salaries with no kids (I think they call that DINK- Dual Income No Kids here in the U.S.) to one salary with a kid and understanding that we wanted to grow our family.

It was a new place, even farther from our families in Puerto Rico and Texas. On top of this, the decision for me to take this role and us deciding that my hubby was going to be a stay-at-home dad was heavily questioned by some members of my family. From a cultural perspective, the fact that the "Dad" wanted to stay at home with the kids was very odd for them. I know as years go by, this is more and more common, but even when we made the decision, it was not the norm, which I think is why I was not able to see a lot of working mothers getting to high roles in management when I first started my career. Later with time, my family ended up understanding and supporting us 100%.

Looking back, I know this decision was not easy on my husband. He joked about how lucky he was to have a "sugar mamma," but I know inside this was a very difficult thing for him to do to adapt from being a very outgoing, growing professional to staying at home entertaining, changing, and feeding the kids.

I am truly lucky and grateful for having the partner and husband that I have. I am also lucky to have these types of "what if" conversations with him even before we got married, because this move was one of the scenarios we discussed many years before it happened, and we knew how we would adapt if it came true. Still, this transition came a bit harder than we expected at the time.

In my role as their site head, I had a bit of additional boundaries to ensure we were in place when it came to making relationships and friendships at the site. To best describe it, it was a bit lonely, but it was an exciting new chapter, and we were up for it.

TROUBLE IN PARADISE

"If there is a problem, yo I'll solve it."—VANILLA ICE

One thing I learned about taking this role was to always ask great questions to know the good, the bad, and the ugly before accepting any role. I did NOT do that for this one. I was so excited about the promotion and opportunity that I was just asking questions about the role description, and that was about it.

From the moment I walked into those doors, I faced challenge after challenge. From cars getting broken into, theft of thousands of dollars, police being called because of threats, and overall a ton of in-depth issues in all parts of operations. On top of that, now this was my responsibility, and all the important letters that I was receiving were addressed to "Dear Ms. Jennifer Lopez." I remember thinking, 'What in the world did I say yes to?' Lesson learned! I now know to ask good questions before I say yes to any opportunity that comes my way.

At the same time, with challenges comes learning, and I always said that if I ever write a book about my career, this chapter would be one of my favorite ones. Because of this challenging assignment, I grew up exponentially as a leader during the five years that I was there, and I am forever grateful for every single challenge that helped me learn.

I started approaching the role the way I approached any new role in the past. First, I would meet with the prior leader for a couple of weeks of transition. Well, there was no prior leader, and the position had been vacant for a month prior to me taking the role.

My backup plan was to ask the other leaders. Unfortunately, most of the information was and stayed with the prior leader, and the functions knew very little of any objectives, plans, or each other.

The backup of the backup plan was to read the documentation of the operations. Well, guess what? There was little to no documentation, at least not the one I was used to in any role in my company. I quickly realized that I had to adapt and approach this role very differently, and had to be creative on how to come up with a strategy very quickly.

Even with the challenges, there was one key asset that this place had, and it was its people. I had the incredible pleasure of meeting and working with incredible people, peers, and friends. They truly had the best "we can" or "we will figure out" attitude I had experienced in my career. In this role, I learned the value of having the diversity of thought.

Once I established an organizational structure, it was time to quickly work on the strategy and focus on our remediation journey. I was about to start implementing a series of detailed standards from my company, and I was thinking to myself, 'There is no way this site can do this with the small number of resources that they have.' However, I did not share my thoughts, and I laid the requirements to our leadership team, and they quickly showed remarkable positivism and assured me that there would be no problem with implementation.

I was very curious about their optimism and asked

about their thinking regarding their implementation. And everyone had a very well-thought-out working plan for it.

I realized I was biased, because I only had experience with one way around the HOW to implement such requirements. In reality, as long as you are compliant, there are a ton of different ways you can approach anything.

I loved this site's creativity, which opened my eyes to always approaching problems with a very open mindset because otherwise, you will be missing out on creativity and new ideas that can help you easily adapt to your course. By leveraging everyone's strengths, prioritizing, and focusing on our course towards operational excellence, we built a very strong and efficient plan that led us not only to compliance but also to growth in the following five years!

I WILL FIGURE THIS OUT!

"A resourceful person will always make an opportunity fit his or her needs."—NAPOLEON HILL

As a mentor or coach, I have seen people struggle because they do not think they are very smart or they do not know it all. When I start asking questions to best understand where they are coming from, it is a very similar situation. They feel that because they are not the ones coming up with the ideas all the time, they are "failing."

If I am honest here with you, I, too, felt like that early in my career. I even took a personal assessment and one of the classifications was one named "PLANT." That classification meant that you were the idea generator of the team. Well, I had very little PLANT in my assessment, and I took that result as a failure. However, if I had reflected on my strengths more, I would have realized early in my career that I was a great CONNECTOR and SHAPER (molding things and executing them).

In the end, it is about understanding where we play in the diversity of the team. You don't want a team that all excel at being PLANTS because nothing would be implemented. Similarly, if everyone is a great SHAPER, we would not be a very innovative team. This is why it is so important to figure out the strengths of your team members. This way, you can ensure to have the diversity you need to thrive.

A huge skill that is an enormous asset in this world is RESOURCEFULNESS. However, we either do not know what it means, or we take it for granted. Being resourceful is the ability to find and use available resources to solve problems and achieve goals.

As you read the description of my role, you can imagine how lost I felt during those first weeks at work. I did second guess myself and started asking if perhaps accepting this position was one of the worst decisions. I started doubting my readiness for the role. However, I caught myself and started to focus on how I was going to figure it out.

I knew it was time to INVEST in my relationships, my team, and myself. Let me start with the relationships. I knew my team and local resources were extremely small or did not exist. I started doing an inventory of the areas where we needed subject matter expertise (in both consulting and doing the work). Being resourceful meant understanding that we had a ton of that expertise back in our main corporate areas, articulating the needs, influencing to get the help we needed, prioritizing the game plan, and pacing the activities. I also invested locally, where we needed local key capabilities to address our urgent needs.

Then I moved to INVESTING on my team. Some players in the team were new to leadership roles, and others were new to learning about other areas of the site. On top of this, everything was new to them, and there was a ton of skepticism on the team.

Together, we aligned on investing in our leadership skills, teamwork, and expertise. How did we do this? We had a well-being/engagement plan that we put together for our team and the entire site. Every leader would take a turn to create and lead the activities in the year. We had a ton of fun with many activities, including office hours, cookouts, a dessert competition, family games/picnic day, a costume competition, office yoga, scavenger hunts, and many more.

We also improved the investment in our team's learning plans and training. As a leadership team, we also invested in our leadership skills and had a quarterly leadership education plan where we focused on improving as a team.

Last but not least, I INVESTED in myself. I knew that taking this role was going to require a ton of strategic thinking. I identified three ways to improve my skills on this subject:

- Identified senior leaders in the company that were the best at strategy and asked them if they could be my mentors.
- Identified training that I could take and books that I could read to continue to improve.
- Identified a project that would be the best "head dunk" approach for me to learn by doing.

Let me talk a bit more about that last one. I love to advise people to drive their careers and be on the lookout for opportunities. In other words, don't just sit and wait for things to happen.

At this point in my role, I knew I needed something big to continue growing. There was a strategic project taking place, and I asked to be the leader of it. The senior leader of that area asked me, "But Jennie, what do you know about strategic planning?" I responded, 'That's exactly the piece I must learn. However, I am a great project manager, certified black belt, and know my site the best from everyone you have on the team, so far. If you set me up with a mentor from your team, I know that I will leverage my learning agility to successfully execute the project. By giving me this opportunity, you will help me to continue to grow as a leader in the company.' Ladies and gentlemen, yes, I got the strategic project leadership role!

Invest does not have to mean money all the time. You can invest in resources that you have at your fingertips. You can invest in relationships. You have what you need to accomplish anything you want, and you don't have to do it alone. Identify the areas that you need to continue to strengthen. Then, identify the resources you have. Last but not least, INVEST.

BEST VIDEO CALL CATCH!

"If you only walk on sunny days, you'll never reach your destination."—PAULO COELHO

This journey towards remediation was not easy. So many things needed to be remediated and improved in parallel to delivering normal day-to-day operations. I had never worked so hard before that role. It was "all hands on deck," working nonstop day and night.

I was thankful that I lived six minutes away from the site, and knowing that my husband was at home with the baby gave me the peace of mind I needed for those days of constant work.

On the flip side, this also created a bad habit for me. I did not stop working! I would go early to work, work until late, come back for late dinner, put the baby to bed, and open my laptop again at home, and work until after midnight.

One afternoon, I was in my office doing a video call with my HR business partner, who was in another state, and in the middle of the call, she looked at me strangely and said, "What is that on your neck?" and I looked at her a bit confused, and replied, 'What do you mean? I don't have anything on my neck.' She described to me what she was seeing, and I started touching my neck, still thinking that maybe there was something on her screen, not on me. Then "ouch." I touched a very tender area that looked like a growth on my neck. I did not think any of it, but she insisted on me getting it checked. I had no idea what this "thing" was, but now that I knew about it, it was the only thing I could see and feel.

I called the doctor, and after the description, I got scheduled for a first-in-the-morning appointment the next day. During my appointment, everything escalated very quickly to the possibility of the "c" word you do not want to hear. You can imagine how my worry and anxiety also escalated immediately, thinking the worst, and me having a two-year-old baby girl.

After many x-rays, MRIs, and other external interventions, they could not figure out what it was. All they knew was that it was growing; they did not like the growth's pace and had to remove it.

This "thing" started growing so much that I started calling it my evil twin, using comedy as a coping mechanism. I had two surgeons working with me, a bone cancer surgeon and a cardiovascular surgeon, because of the location of the growth (on my neck, close to my clavicle, and close to a major artery).

They warned me that the surgery was going to be very intrusive because the location and where they had to cut meant that I was going to lose my mobility for a long time, and to prepare myself for a long recovery and a big scar. The scar was the least of my worries at that moment. I just wanted it to be out and was praying that whatever I had was just localized.

At this time, it became extremely clear. I must **invest in myself** and put myself first. I needed to prioritize myself, so I could find myself healthy again for my baby girl and my husband. Time is our most valuable resource. I decided to invest in the best care and ensure that my time was going towards what were the most important people in my life.

Before I had kids, I had a huge concern about not being a good mom because I unintentionally prioritized my work ahead of them. When I had this health issue, it became extremely obvious, and there were no questions asked about what came first. My family was #1! I share this because I do not want anyone to go through a health scare to realize this.

Before the surgery, I asked for two extra weeks because I wanted to return to Puerto Rico for my uncle's wedding. I also wanted to truly disconnect before the big surgery. The doctors thought I was having "cold feet," but ultimately, they were okay with the two-week delay. I worked with my team and supervision, so we had a coverage plan that truly allowed me to 100% disconnect while I was in Puerto Rico and during surgery recovery time.

For two weeks, I truly enjoyed every moment without any work-related worry. I tried very hard not to think about my evil twin, and instead focused on the fact that we were going to remove it and I was going to be recovering soon. Remember, "WHERE FOCUS GOES, ENERGY FLOWS."

Some people called it luck; I attributed it to the "magic waters of Puerto Rico," but by the time I returned home to get ready for my surgery, the growing growth was almost nonexistent. I called the doctors again and shared, "I do not think I need the surgery anymore." They really thought I was just scared and rushed me to the office to see me. To everyone's surprise, it was gone. The area was not tender anymore; the growth was not visible. They said it was up to me at this point, and I decided to keep an eye on it but not to proceed with the surgery.

If you are curious about what was the cause of my "evil twin," let's then fast forward three years. I am now back in Indianapolis in another role, and there it goes, the same story repeated. The same worry, but now with the regret that I did not do anything for three years—and now it could be something worse, and I now have a four-year-old girl and a new baby boy.

The same number of X-rays, MRIs, and other inconclusive tests followed. Back to two new surgeons and a new surgery scheduled. It was the week before the surgery, and they ordered one more X-ray to prepare for the surgical approach and location in a more precise way.

Thank God for the curiosity of this X-ray technician. He kept looking at it, and said that it was very odd and strongly recommended that I go to this surgeon at the children's hospital.

At this point, his persistence made me think that maybe I could get another opinion and new answers. I met the surgeon, and he said that he had not seen it in adults, but usually they detect it in kids and correct it. I cannot remember the actual term, but it was a part of the vein that separated like a bubble, and when it experienced high pressure (aka stress), it would blow like a balloon putting pressure on other veins.

I finally had answers! Knowing this, I knew I had to

manage my stress. This clearly explains the magic waters of Puerto Rico phenomenon. Once again, once the stress went down, so did my "evil twin," and I did not proceed with surgery.

I learned my lesson. Intentionally eliminate stress! It's obviously easier said than done, but something I focus on and strive to be proactive about it. Now you know, if you start seeing my "evil twin," please let me know!

Let's go back to this lesson. Do you express stress in your life? Do you know how harmful stress can be if left unchecked? It can cause many health problems, including high blood pressure, obesity, diabetes, and heart disease. These health issues are sneaky and come when you least expect them.

The good thing is that you can be proactive about it! What small changes can you make to eliminate stress? Workout? Vacation time? Monthly massages? Reading a book without distractions? Write a list of at least five options and start this week with one of them! Do it for you and for the people around you. Trust me; it is the best personal investment!

WHAT TRULY MATTERS

"Time has a wonderful way of showing us what really matters."—MARGARET PETERS

This was a very scary way of learning. I share this with you because I would hate for you to go through a painful or scary health situation because of not having the right priorities or integration in life. Many times, we hear similar stories and say, "Oh, but I'm ok, that will not happen to me," thinking we are untouchable. I know I did think this way and boom! It showed up when I least expected it.

Going through this taught me what truly matters in life. I go back to what my work colleague said, wanting to be remembered as the best dad in the world and not the best scientist in the world. My family is *numero uno,* and will always be!

I had to go back to my personal mission and purpose in my career. I wanted to become that role model that I did not have. I did not want to show that the only way to make it happen was to "kill ourselves" and be burned out. This period of recalibration and adaptation was key in how I approached my career and leadership. I will tell you it was not easy, but my WHY and purpose were louder than the excuses.

We working mothers carry an extra burden and pressure of thinking that we need to be everything for everyone. We feel the need to fit the role of the perfect mother, daughter, leader, friend, employee, caregiver, and perfect everything.

However, perfection is a goal that is impossible to ever achieve. This is why we feel the guilt of not being good enough and feel that we are failing at everything. That's too much, my friends! And what is the good thing about living a life like this? I do not see any bright side, so we need to flip this around and have a different mindset.

I look back at some of the many opinions that have been shared with me out of a "caring" place, and I now chuckle a bit. However, I can see how comments can truly mess with your mind.

For example, when my daughter was born, I lived in a neighborhood where most of the women were stay-at-home mothers, and they once shared with me at one of the ladies' gatherings while the men were playing poker at another house: "Jennie, we just feel bad that you have to work!" I was surprised by the question and said, 'Wait, what? I HAVE to work? I WANT to work!' I tried to explain it, but they were not getting it. Their reality was a very different one from mine. The next thing I did was text my husband, "Please get me out of here!"

I also had a senior leader who once said, "You know what, Jennie? I see women like you, and I feel bad. I think society is doing such a bad job making you all feel like you have to work." And my friends, this was not that long ago.

Once again, I tried to explain to him that I really wanted to work and loved my career, but he was not keeping track of me. I am sure he thought I was brainwashed by society.

Add to these comments others like, "Wow, you travel so much, I am sure you feel guilty about leaving your kids alone at home," "I cannot believe you missed your daughter's first dance recital," "Don't you rather stay at home with your baby so you don't miss their milestones," and many more.

The best thing I did was not to let these comments mess with my mind and make a reality with my OWN and personal definition of what it meant being the best mom for my kids.

We also need to understand that everyone's perspectives will be different based on their upbringing, experiences, values, and personal framework. Instead of me thinking, 'How dare he say that? I can't believe she said that to me,' I learned that they probably shared those things out of care based on their own reality. However, other people's reality does not have to define yours!

Think about it. We strive to be a perfect mother (or perfect parent). But in reality, what does that even mean? If you ask 100 people to define what it means to be a "perfect mother/parent," you will receive more than 100 different responses meaning that if you try to be each of those definitions, you are approaching mission impossible. Who do you need to prove anything to? Only your children deserve that amount of focus and energy, not the rest of society.

Instead, define YOUR personal goal on how you want to be that awesome mother/parent for your kids. For example, I decided that I wanted my kids to have meaningful memories. I know this may sound to some of you like a Hallmark e-card, but it is truly something so simple yet powerful—and it makes perfect sense to me.

I want my kids to be supported and loved. I want them to experience things that make them learn and grow to be good human beings. I want to be a good role model showing them that life is not an EITHER/OR situation, and you can live with an "AND" mindset to live the life that you dream of. I want them to see me as a coach when needed, and know that I will be there when they need me. I want them to be independent and live a life that they choose, and not one that is limited or chosen for them.

See how I am not mentioning here that I want them to live in a house that is 100% clean at all times, or to have a mom that bakes goodies for school, or have a mom that does not miss any single dance practice or activity, or a mom that feeds them veggies with every meal? I am picking my battles! I aim to stay away from absolutes because that is not a formula for success. The key for me is how to integrate all different aspects of my life to be the best I can be so I can be at my best for everyone I love and care for.

I chose to be driven by my big picture statement of my kids having memorable memories, and I am perfectly okay with HOW I do it, because it is my own definition and nobody else's. In the same way, I cheer for all other moms who do amazing things for their kids based on their own definitions.

We need to rally for each other instead of judging or tearing each other apart. We have enough pressure in this world and do not need this type of constant feeling that we are not doing our job "right" based on others' definitions or expectations.

Mamis: Let's support each other and embrace our mami-unicorns to continue thriving in life and become the best we can be.

Going back to the importance of investing here... Once you have that goal in mind, then you can start thinking about how to invest to take you closer to living that goal. For example, are there activities you need to outsource to make your goal a reality? Are there family members, friends, or caregivers that can give you a break so you can focus on yourself? Are there podcasts or books that can keep you updated on how to raise kids these days?

If you are a parent, please pause here to reflect and try it. Remember not to overcomplicate it. What is YOUR definition of SUCCESS as a parent? What is YOUR goal? Is this new/optimized goal modifying the way you are approaching parenting? How can you continue to invest in your parenting goal?

If you just skipped this chapter thinking it does not apply to you because you are not a parent, please reread it and think about how it applies to you. Is there anything you do that "society" has some norms as to how that should look or perform? Ignore that noise and focus on what is YOUR personal goal and INVEST towards getting you closer to that goal!

Chapter Key Takeaways:

- **SET YOUR BOUNDARIES**—A big ADAPT key takeaway from the experiences I shared with you is prioritizing what matters the most to you.

In my case, my family. Since I talked a lot about setting boundaries that make sense for YOU, I wanted to share a few that have worked for me as a working mother in case it helps you or inspires you to draft new for you! Here are a few:

- Choose your workplace thoughtfully and ensure it aligns with your values.
- Build trust with your supervisor, share your personal priorities, and align on expectations.
- Proactively block meaningful time for your kids (e.g., key school activities, lunch dates, key extracurricular activities, etc.).
- Proactively schedule fun and surprise activities with your family.

- Have a game plan with your tribe (e.g., driving the kids, homework time, house chores, etc.).
- Outsource when you can (e.g., cleaning, maintenance activities, cooking, lawn, etc.).
- Do not reinforce unwanted behaviors (e.g., answering late-night emails, saying yes to everything).
- Own your time! Be very intentional about what you say YES to.
- Understand you cannot be everywhere every time. Give yourself grace. Choose your battles or as I say, choose your winnings! Think big picture, will this specific moment impact what I want for my family?
- Ask for help! It takes an army, and it is 100% okay to ask for help.
- Set a structure where it makes sense. Be clear and specific.
- Designate "workplace" and ensure you put a time framework during the "workplace" and intentional time with the kiddos.
- Write down yearly family objectives. Be clear and specific. Track them, make them happen, and enjoy the outcome!

- **INVEST IN YOURSELF**—Sometimes we do so much for other people that we forget the most important one: OURSELVES! For example, we tend to always seek out how we can help our families. For those of us who are parents, we want the best for our kids, investing in their school, extracurricular activities, development experience, and future.

However, when it comes to us, we tend to say things like, 'I'm ok, I don't need it,' 'I don't have time,' 'It is too expensive,' 'I don't deserve it,' ta da da da da da (Spanish for blah blah blah). Remember what we discussed before in the book: "When you prioritize yourself, you prioritize everyone you love."

Here are ways to intentionally invest in your personal and career development:

- Prioritize time for you and be proactive in your learning: there are many platforms at your fingertips (work-provided platforms, YouTube, free seminars, books, LinkedIn Learning, and others).
- Be on the lookout for trainings and or conferences that will help you grow in your role. Ask your leadership for support!
- Involve your leadership in the process of identifying mentors.

- Identify key networking groups or activities within your scope of work or personal focus area.
- Put yourself in new leadership opportunities that can continue to grow you as a leader (e.g., boards, advisory councils, ERGs/BRGs (Employee Resource Groups/Business Resource Groups), school boards, church, small groups, etc.)
- Invest in a personal coach.
- Invest in your well-being!

1. DRAW YOUR BOUNDARIES
2. INVEST IN YOURSELF

Chapter 7

CREATE

"But what part of me do I choose?"

Have you ever seen and admired some people and their accomplishments? Perhaps you thought, 'That will never be me because (fill the blank).' Well, let's change that perspective a little bit. Your life is not determined by your past, what other people think, your education, or your financial status. You have the power inside of you to **CREATE** the experiences and path that you dream of.

In this chapter, I share the pivotal time in my career when I went from feeling trapped to moving forward with purpose. I also share an awesome mindset tool and the importance of knowing that you don't have to do it alone!

WORK HARD, PEOPLE WILL NOTICE = FALSE ADVERTISEMENT!

"You can do anything as long as you have the passion, the drive, the focus, and the support."—SABRINA BRYAN

My growing career and personal journey was one that I will never forget. Looking back, I am grateful because, from that challenge, I grew exponentially. I grew as a person, a mom, and as a leader.

After almost five years in that role, I started to evaluate my next career options. At that time, I had spent half of my career in one division of the company and the other half in another one still in manufacturing. I had a choice to continue growing in this recent business unit, but my goal was to get back to the area where I felt a much stronger personal connection.

My decision was not very popular and, some people even told me, "If you go back to the other division, it will take you three times the amount of time to get to where you want to be instead of staying here." I listened to them, but at the same time, I was thinking that I would not have any problem continuing to grow in management, since my results would speak for themselves.

I just wrote "my results would speak for themselves" but inside of me, I'm screaming, 'STOP BRAGGING, JENNIE!' But please stay with me here, because this "authentic confidence" is a very important topic I will cover later in the book!

I got a leadership role in a new plant where I felt a much stronger connection. This role was exciting, and we were responsible for the company's top products and future ones.

After just a few weeks in the role I realized what they meant when they said, "It will take you three times the amount of time to get where you want to be." It was a new world and all new people and senior leaders from when I left. The good thing is that the role was exciting, and I said to myself, 'No biggie... you have done this many times, new place, learn it, lead and perform.' I decided to put my head down and work hard.

"Work hard, and people will notice" is a very common saying, and teaching that many of us were raised with. That's exactly what I did; I worked very hard so people would notice. I wanted to make them proud. I wanted to ensure that they felt they made a good decision by choosing me for this role. I thought that they were taking a chance on me by bringing me to this role, where I had no previous experience, vs. all other leaders who were "born and raised" in this plant and platform.

I prioritized my job and only my job in my engineering career world. I had other opportunities coming my way, but I declined them. I was asked to lead the Organization of Latinos, and I told them I had no time. The Women in

Leadership Association asked for my help to lead a board pillar, and I also declined because I was too busy. Everything outside of my work bubble was a NO. Networking events? NO, After-hours social events? NO. Volunteering work? NO. You get the point. I started drawing a very black and white way of defining what was my only work scope.

Outside of my professional work, my love for dancing had transformed into a continuing career. I was honored to be selected as a master trainer/education specialist working for a globally popular dance fitness company.

I loved every single minute of it. I continued doing what I loved and educating other instructors to spread the knowledge, talent, and passion about healthy living. I was filling my cup intentionally.

Some people called me crazy because of all of my "jobs," but once again, I truly enjoyed every single one of them on top of having a great time with my toddler kids and making fun memories. Somehow, I found a way to integrate it all and still had the boundaries that each aspect of my life required.

A TOY FROM THE ISLAND OF MISFIT TOYS

"If you desire to make a difference in the world, you must be different from the world."—ELAINE S. DALTON

Do you remember the "Rudolph the Red-Nosed Reindeer " movie? In that movie, there is a scene where they walk to the "island of misfit toys." In that island, there are many toys out there that were not found "fit" for the children because they were different and had "flaws," if you compared them with the "normal" toys.

For example, there was a choo-choo train with square wheels; a bird that did not fly and instead liked to swim; an elephant with pink dots; and many others. These toys did not fit the mold; therefore, they were ignored and were left alone, and labeled as misfits.

Sadly, I got to a time in my life where that is exactly how I felt. I was a toy that did not fit the mold, and was ignored on an island. I felt like no matter what I did, I was not going to be good enough to fit the mold. By mold, I mean a box-like standard that people had for what GOOD was and SUCCESS looked and felt like.

I started feeling like a unicorn in a race of horses. My internal dialogue was out of control: 'What am I doing there? Why am I different? How can I hide this horn? I don't want it! How can I cover it up? Being a horse is the only way I could accomplish my goals... I need to be a horse!'

In the dance/fitness world, some colleagues constantly questioned my craft because this job was a part-time job for me and not the full-time career that the majority had. My fifteen years of experience (at that time) as a certified fitness instructor didn't matter—and many more years of experience as a professional dancer. I had to always prove myself, always feeling the pressure to perform at 200% to prove that I deserved to be part of this amazing company like everyone else. And yet, it was not enough to get the cool opportunities other people were getting.

In the engineering/professional career world, I had to prove myself every single time, no matter how great my outcomes were. I continued to get very superficial feedback like, "We need to make sure that you are technical," "You seem too nice. Can you handle difficult conversations?," "You empower your employees too much" (actually, for this one, I said 'you are welcome' because I thought they were complimenting me until I realized that they meant it as an area for improvement), "Your leadership style is different and until it changes they will always question you," "You handle your role like this is a democracy, you need to make all the calls by yourself," "You keep highlighting other people, are they doing the work or are you doing the work?" "If you want to continue to grow as a serious leader, you will have to quit the "dancy" job you have."

Seriously, all of this made no sense to me. I did have a different leadership style, but that was my secret sauce because it was the way I connected with my teams. I enabled trust and focused on people development, organization growth, and engagement. In return, the results spoke louder than anything else.

However, that is not how it had been done before. Yes, I was nice, but because I CARED! That did not make me a weak leader. Actually, it was quite the opposite; it made me a much stronger and more influential leader. And yes, of course, I had to deal with many difficult conversations. It has been the basic nature of the roles that I have had. However, it was questioned if people did not see me in action.

At this point, I continued to be me. I would acknowledge the feedback and work on what needed to be worked on, but when it came to the feedback around my leadership style, I paused. I realized that I needed to become more confident in my own element because I had the personal mission of becoming the role model that I didn't have. At the same time, the need to continue to prove myself on and on and on was exhausting.

Did you ever go to a pool when you were younger, and together with the other kids, you would go in a circle to create a current? Now imagine you were that kid trying to go against the current. Remember the feeling of trying very hard with all you had but barely being able to move? That's exactly how I felt, and unfortunately, I know this is not a unique situation.

For me, I did not realize how discouraged and hopeless I was feeling until my husband one time after work asked me, "How are you?" and I said, "Fine," and then he asked me again, "No, really, how are you? You don't seem to want to talk about your work anymore. You lost your spark." At that point, I thought, "What are you talking about?" Quickly after that, I had tears on my face. "You are so right. I'm not happy. I feel trapped," I thought. Here I thought I was doing such a great job at hiding my internal dilemma, so I could still be a strong wife and mom for my family, but it was obviously starting to impact my personal life.

BUT WHAT PART OF ME DO I CHOOSE?

"Some people want it to happen, some wish it would happen, others make it happen."—MICHAEL JORDAN

I felt unsupported and lost. Now, I was mid-career and really did not see the light at the end of the tunnel. I thought that maybe if I chose one area to "show" and "prove" that I was dedicated, I would be able to get to the goals I wanted to achieve. I thought that I either had to stop my dancing/fitness career or this engineering career that was going nowhere in my mind. This choice and decision that I thought I HAD to make was breaking me inside.

Each role I had was feeding a side of me. One on

the creative side, the other on the technical side, and the combination of both: the business side. But how do I choose? What side of me do I choose? I felt like if I chose one, I would miss the other one terribly and somehow lose that piece of the puzzle that made me who I was.

I have learned that when I have all of these crazy thoughts in my mind, the best way to really think them through is by writing them down and talking to someone. Writing things down allows a higher level of thinking, which helps you with more focused actions. When your brain is not busy processing everything, you can allow time to analyze and ask great questions.

When it came to talking to someone, I wanted to reach out to someone that could somehow understand what I was going through with both careers. I quickly thought of a great mentor that I had (and still have!) that was a chemical engineer and had an incredible career in different companies and sectors. He was also an executive leader at the same fitness company that I was working at. I am so happy I reached out to him, because he told me something I will never forget. This was the first foundational a-ha moment in my personal transformational journey.

As I shared my dilemma and told him that I needed to choose and did not know which one, he quickly said, "WHY NOT BOTH?" (Sound familiar? This was exactly my response when I was eighteen years old). I told him, "That's exactly what I have been doing, but I think it is actually playing against me?" Then he said something that was PURE GOLD:

- **"Do you realize that each side of you is making the other one stronger?"**

He was sooooo right! I had the confidence to work with teams because of my multiple years of teaching and presenting as a dancer and fitness professional. I had a great dance fitness business because of my organization, engineering skills, attention to detail, learning agility, and a tendency for problem-solving. The charisma and personal branding that I own comes from the person that I have become, influenced by the experiences that I have had.

It all comes down to interpretation. In my mind, my STORY (the one I was telling myself) was that "this is playing against me." I let other people's feedback get to me, so it turned it into my BELIEF. That BELIEF drove my ACTIONS, and they started playing against me because the RESULTS were not encouraging.

This is a very important concept! We need to own the stories we tell ourselves because they feed the cycle that yields our results. If this cycle is empowering, that is awesome because it will continue to grow stronger and stronger. However, if this cycle is disempowering, it will take you down quickly in a spiral.

Here is the formula:
STORY → BELIEF → ACTIONS → RESULTS

- What is the **STORY** you are telling yourself?
- From that STORY, what **BELIEFS** have you developed?
- From those BELIEFS, what **ACTIONS** have you taken?
- What have been the **RESULTS** from your ACTIONS?

For me, this belief of me feeling like I did not fit anywhere was playing against me and started to become a vicious cycle that was not helping anyone involved. Instead, with what my mentor shared, I realized a different story in front of me! The fact that I had these different personal elements was my COMPETITIVE ADVANTAGE! I needed to be intentional with this to work at my best, serve at my best, and drive my journey with authenticity, passion, and confidence. This is the magic that you can CREATE by having empowering stories and beliefs.

My mentor probably does not know how those words impacted me. His way of believing in and supporting me has impacted my life! Many times, it takes only ONE PERSON to validate the steps that you are taking and give you that pivotal push that helps you fly confidently to your next chapter.

Really think about it; every aspect of our lives makes the other ones stronger. If we live intentionally with this in mind, we will be unstoppable! Now imagine that at work, everyone shows up with the same intention. Imagine that instead of people minimizing themselves and hiding certain elements of themselves, they show up with not only their unique selves but their amplified and intentional persona.

"Your Stories Drive Your Results"

You would have an energized team of unicorns ready to tackle every challenge and make the impossible a reality.

Try now to reflect on this and think about all the sides of you. How are they making you a stronger individual? How can you use that intentionally to CREATE the journey, experiences, and impact you want?

YOU DON'T HAVE TO DO IT ALONE!

"When the student is ready, the teacher will appear."
—BUDDHA

Well, as you can imagine, I did not choose one... I CHOSE BOTH! Once I had that realization, I was fueled by purpose, and I was determined to figure out the next steps.

I have learned that the times when I get stuck or anxious because I don't even know how to proceed with the next steps because of two things:

1) Lack of clarity
2) Feeling that I am on my own

They go hand in hand. We discussed the importance of deciding, committing, taking action, adapting, and investing.

Without **clarity**, you are driving with a blindfold. The sooner you have clarity about where you want to go, the sooner you can start working on your game plan. You can create many paths, experiences, and outcomes in life if you have clarity. Clarity is what helps you find focus, and direction will help you move forward.

Still, we sometimes get trapped with our thoughts and think we need to figure everything out by ourselves. But guess what? WE DON'T. **We do not have to do it alone!** Life is full of students and teachers. Each of us is a student and teacher at different stages of our lives and in different aspects of our lives. I'm a huge believer that we are here on this planet to serve others. We never stop learning. When we stop learning, we stop creating. Mentors, sponsors, coaches... We need them all!

Going back to my story. I reached out to my mentors: internal to the company and external. I even connected with the people who were my mentors earlier in my career and since then have retired. I CREATED new connections with leaders from other parts of the company and peers that I knew I could trust. I expanded my network as I had never done it before. If I am honest, the greatest benefit from my expanded network was CONFIDENCE. These people saw things in me that I didn't even see myself.

You may be thinking: "Okay, Jennie... GOT IT! We need mentors, sponsors, and coaches. But what is the difference? Aren't they all the same?"

Here is how I love to explain it (something I heard once that stuck with me, and I expanded on it a bit). Imagine that you have a big, awesome-looking, shiny door in front of you. On the other side of that door is that next big opportunity that you are working for!

- **MENTOR**—Shows you the door, describes the door with you, shares their experiences with the doors (what worked, what didn't work), and accelerates your learning path to get closer to that door.
- **SPONSOR**—Has seen you in action, and when you are ready, "Opens the door for you!"
- **PROFESSIONAL COACH**—They are with you at every step of your journey before and after the door to give you unbiased coaching, from mindset to executive skills.

When you have a great mentor, sponsor, or coach, you know it because you have an immediate connection based on trust, and they make you feel understood and empowered. They help you get the clarity you need about the next steps in your journey!

VISIBILITY IS KEY!

"The power of visibility can never be underestimated."
—MARGARET CHO

The feeling of invisibility is very common in minority talent. I, too, felt invisible, especially when I got to be a mid-career professional. It is the feeling of not being seen, not feeling appreciated, and being taken for granted. The feeling of being skipped because we do not fit the norm.

I once took leadership training that taught me something very impactful, and I want to share it with you here. It was about the power of visibility. When you start your career, working hard will make you one of the top performers. Because of being a top performer, you will continue to grow organically, until a certain point. At this point, everyone with you is there because they also worked hard and were top performers.

This is where things like sponsorship, visibility, and intentionality behind your strengths (personal brand) come into play. I want to talk about visibility because that is the piece I struggled with the most.

Remember when I shared with you that I started to say NO to everything outside my scope of work? I was getting so immersed in my bubble that I started to become invisible by my own decisions.

You may think that if you do a great job, results should speak for themselves, and everything else is just corporate politics (I know I did!). Well, I have learned that is a bit of human nature too. We all have unconscious biases and tend to make decisions with what we know and experience.

The same goes for hiring decisions. If all are the same (credentials, experience, etc.), there is a tendency to hire who you know and have had experience with, because you think you know what you will get. I am not saying that is right or wrong, just stating a natural bias we all have and need to be on the lookout for.

This is why being visible is so important. Do people know you or know of you? If they don't know you well, you can become just a name on a piece of paper. Instead, the focus should be on how you can increase your visibility authentically, not in a "look at me" way.

For example, I asked myself these questions: 'Where else can I add value? What is an area that I am passionate about? Where can I help that will develop me and also gives me some proximity with key leaders in the organization?' My answers became very clear; it was the Latinx ERG

(Employee Resource Group) at my company. I joined their board and volunteered to lead the pillar focused on developing and accelerating our Latinx talent.

It was the best decision ever! Not only did I connect with so many wonderful friends, but I also worked on something super impactful. I was helping our community in a time of much need. The side benefit was that many leaders saw me leading in action. I started to get visibility while doing something that I was passionate about!

Now, if visibility is something you can improve on, what actions can you take? Do you have mentors that can help you? Can you set a meeting with your supervisor to come up with a game plan together? Can you volunteer for special projects? Is there a short-term assignment that you can benefit from? You have options!

THERE IS NOTHING WRONG WITH ME

"Do not diminish who you are. Your gender, your heritage, your identity. That's what makes you unique."—KAILIN GOW

Growing up in the corporate world, I always had a nagging feeling that there was something wrong with me. No matter what I did to fit in, it was obvious that it was not enough, and I still felt like I stood out for the wrong reasons. As I started to realize the value I bring with my uniqueness and the very diverse experiences that I had, I also had another BIG a-ha moment.

Around this time in my career, the topic of employee journeys and research about different minority groups' experiences in the workplace started to surface everywhere. I even participated in some of these research exercises and read extensively on this topic. This was when I realized with a HUGE side of relief. I get it! **There is absolutely nothing wrong with me! Most of the feedback I received was very linked to the personal and leadership characteristics wired in me from my Latin heritage and upbringing.**

I am very proud of my LATINA roots, and there is nothing wrong with my leadership style. But see, it was very different from what had been seen in the corporate world. For many years, the workplace composition was very homogeneous and what was deemed successful felt and looked a certain way.

The definition of what a successful leader should be like, dress like, speak like, behave like, could fit in a box. Anything different from that box is not trusted because, again, that is now how things have been done before. I realized that the feedback that I was receiving perhaps came with good intent (I am trying to give the benefit of the doubt to many of my previous leaders). I had been coached to be more like that box, so I, too, could be successful.

This is exactly where I disagree with many "women's leadership" or "minority leadership" programs out there; they try to teach us to be more like the box, so we can move the needle.

I have a friend that was told how to dress, how to have her hair done, and nails painted to be in leadership. I have received training on how to speak, act like the "boys," behave, and exercise my leadership so I could be taken seriously and grow on the corporate ladder. This is where I want to scream from the top of my lungs and say that enough is enough, and **"IT IS TIME TO BREAK THIS CRAZY CYCLE OF CREATING MORE OF THE SAME AVATAR-LIKE LEADERS!"**

I also want to say that we need to be extremely grateful for those minority leaders before us. In my case, I see these very few Latinas in executive roles, and I know their journey was even more difficult than mine. I know that to get there, they had to play by the "corporate unspoken rules" to get to the position of influence and power to make meaningful change.

At the same time, now we are growing so fast that we need to start embracing the true beauty of diversity and change the rules of the game. We have the numbers! Now we need to work together with confidence and 100% intention. Changing the rules of the game is not only to benefit us; it will benefit everyone involved. Richer diversity in the workplace yields better culture, true innovation, acceleration of results, and much better outcomes for the people we serve. We need to CREATE a culture where true diversity is the norm.

What we bring to the table may be different, but let me tell you, it brings a ton of value and energy to the organization. Let's take, for example, my feedback on bubbliness, too high energy, engaging too much with my employees, being too nice, having "too much fun," too cross-functional, not too direct, etc.

That's how I was raised in Puerto Rico. We do everything as a team, celebrate the little wins and the big ones, and have fun even when we are working through the toughest challenges. We lead with a "we," not "I," because in the end, we all work towards the same goal to win together. This leadership style has been what has helped me connect with everyone at any level and has helped me create the highest engaged teams that end up having top performance results.

The key is to also recognize that every strength we have, if we overuse it, could also bring some derailers into the equation. In other words, we must watch how overusing some of our strengths can play against us. The strength may be already unique to the people around you; use it wisely and intentionally, so it does play for you instead of against you.

For example, if your "nice" makes you spend too much time making sure everyone agrees or likes you, then you may be too slow at decision-making. If you keep working hard to protect your team, your "family," you may assume that your supervisor will also cheer on you and look after you. Well, that is not the case all the time, and while you are waiting for things to happen, others are driving their careers intentionally with their foot all the way on the pedal.

One last example: We Latinx (Latinos, Latinas) are usually wired to be very good with change management because that has been our lives. We roll with the punches, adapt, and keep going. Well, you may be too fast with change and may not bring everyone along with you because you may assume everyone is wired that way as well.

We all have unique superpowers, but let's also remember that the one thing that we tend to work so hard on minimizing, hiding, or changing is that unique thing that separates us and makes us shine: our HERITAGE! Let's make it shine so we can strengthen it, and the generations to come can confidently continue to amplify it!

Chapter Key Takeaways:

- **EXPAND YOUR NETWORK**—There is a saying that says, "You become the people you surround yourself with; choose carefully." This is why I'm a big believer in expanding your network, so you are not alone and can surround yourself with people that inspire you to be the best version of yourself.

I usually get asked the question about how to find a mentor. In my opinion, there is not a single formula for finding one, but I want to share three points to consider:

- Make sure you both have a good connection based on trust.
- You (mentee) drive it! Be specific on what you want out of the mentorship relationship and what you can provide. A mentorship should add value to everyone involved. Is it for career, skill-specific, cultural aspect, or specific experience?
- Evaluate your mentorships as you grow in your career. Are they still valuable? Do you have different needs? Do you need to elevate the level of exposure?
- I know I said THREE. Here is the bonus: Do not overcomplicate it! Reach out to the person, and if you don't know them, find someone who can establish the link and speak on your behalf? (Supervisor? Friend? Colleague?)

Just for kicks... here is how I have found my mentors:

- Assigned through a mentorship program
- Mentorship circles
- Connected at a business dinner

- Supervisor connection based on my aspirations
- Cold LinkedIn message to a Board of Directors member
- After a conference, she said, "It was a pleasure, feel free to reach out to me if you have any follow up questions." So I did; I emailed her right away.
- Waiting in line at the company coffee shop. I connected with the person next to me, and shared that I was starting a new role in the organization, and shared a bit about my journey. We realized we had a background commonality (similar career change), and he mentioned he wanted to mentor me. I then realized I was talking about finding the organization.
- The leader I was helping as a Black Belt for one of his projects. We continued with a mentorship relationship after the project was completed.
- Coaches from personal growth trainings

Remember, you don't have to do it alone. Treasure these relationships and be intentional with them.

- **CREATE EXPERIENCES**—You have the power to create the experiences that you desire. Have you ever thought that you wish you had "x" job, but don't have the experience? Or perhaps you wanted to create something beautiful like a book, a piece of art, or a podcast, but do not have the experience? This is an example of the importance of being resourceful. First of all, have CLARITY of the overall job or outcome that you desire. What are some skills that you need? How can you develop those skills? How can you CREATE experiences to develop the skills? The key is NOT to remain stagnant. Remember to constantly grow.

Here are a few ideas on how you can CREATE experiences:

- Join external networks
- Volunteer in nonprofit organizations
- Join a board (company, nonprofit, school, etc.)
- Shadow and help people who are already doing what you want to do
- Join and help national or local organizations
- Work intentionally with mentors
- Volunteer at church
- Find a network that can help you grow in the niche that you are looking for
- Look for specific volunteering work related to your niche
- Ask for a specific special assignment at work

You get the idea now. How else can you CREATE experiences to get closer to your goal?

- **COMPLETE YOUR UNICORN**—Let's put your puzzle together. After reading this chapter, do a bit of self-reflection and write down the unique strengths and characteristics that make you, YOU! What are some of your superpowers?

I am also sharing mine today as an example. (Remember that we are evolving unicorns!)

After you CREATE your unicorn, remember that this is the unicorn that, from now on, you will bring with you intentionally into everything you do. Channel your inner unicorn and thrive authentically!

Jennie's Intentional Unicorn

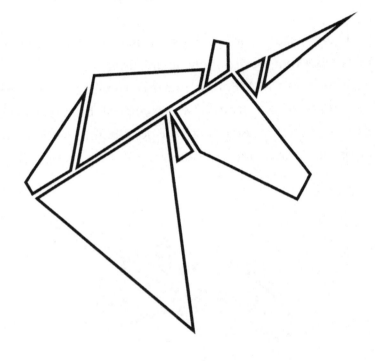

Put your puzzle together, complete your UNICORN!

Chapter 8

AMPLIFY

"Success is Not the Destination"

Have you ever dreamt of one day becoming successful? What does that look like? Have you ever reflected on what it truly means to be successful? Here I share how to look at that word through a different lens. Once you can connect with a more meaningful definition of what SUCCESS is and what it is not, it will help you **AMPLIFY** your impact. This will help not only you but the people around you.

NOT GOOD ENOUGH
"We cannot be all things to all people."—CESAR CONDE

As I kept doing my best and working on the aspects that I recently learned about visibility and sponsorship, I kept receiving this nagging feedback regarding my leadership style. I had a senior leader tell me, "I just don't think you will ever get that promotion because your leadership style is so much different from everyone else that it will just continue to get questioned."

How he shared that like it was just a matter of fact did not sit well with me. I got into a downward spiral, where I felt hopeless and stuck. The best way to describe my feeling was like I was a chip on a board game and my destination and moves were solely in the hands of others. I lost my confidence, my bubbliness, my energy, and my passion.

I was so full of dreams, ambition, drive, energy, and passion, with so much to give, but became sour, powerless, and with a new disempowering mindset of "well, at least I have a job that pays the bills."

I even considered leaving the industry and going back to help coach cheerleading. I started conversations with an NFL team to see what the role would look like and was very close to applying for the director's assistant role.

We live in a society that only celebrates and shines a bright light on successes, but the emotional rollercoaster is not shared because it is perceived as weak. Because of it, we think that there is something wrong with us.

For example, if you see my résumé, bio, or social media, maybe you say, "Wow how cool! Impressive," but you don't see the downs, the disappointments, the many times I closed myself in the work bathroom or office to cry out the anger, the biases, the microaggressions, and the feeling of isolation.

It is time to normalize that the struggle is real and, unfortunately, very common. This is why I decided to write this book, as nerve-racking as it is. I want to share my journey to 1) empathize and say that you are not alone, 2) open your eyes, and 3) inspire action for immediate change.

With time, I have learned that we grow and get to a much better and more evolved place from the struggles; we learn. Think back to a struggle that you had, and now you are in a much better place, or have become a much better person because of it. I am sure there is at least one. That is what "struggles" do, they sharpen your saw and help you become your next amazing version!

ENOUGH IS ENOUGH

"Go where you are celebrated, not tolerated."
—UNKNOWN

I truly love this quote: "Go where you are celebrated, not tolerated." I stayed in one area maybe a bit too long because I was stubborn and wanted to demonstrate that it could be done. At the same time, at what cost?

By being so narrow minded in one specific thing, I was missing the sea of opportunities and the bigger picture lessons I was about to go through. These lessons are now what I continue to share in social media, trainings, coaching, and this book to help as many people as I can.

I thought about changing careers and here are all of the thoughts that came to my mind (I am pouring all of my raw thoughts here, because I am sure some of you are going through this right now):

- Are you going to waste almost 17 years of experience?
- You will have to start from the beginning
- Nobody will know you
- Nobody will want you this late in the game
- You only know one area
- People will think you are a failure
- People will think you are weak
- Minority peers will think that you abandoned them
- What about the people who are looking up to you?
- Your family will be disappointed
- If you are not helping change the culture, who will?
- You are a failure; you did not make it to the role you were dreaming about
- It's too much work; staying here is easy... just go with the flow
- People are going to think you were kicked out

Thank goodness for my rock, my husband. He made me realize that this "disempowered, sour and not confident" person I was becoming was not me.

I wanted to sadly ask myself, 'Jennie, what happened to you?' This is when we have to be careful of the **quality of questions** that we ask ourselves, because if we ask "poopy questions," we get "poopy answers."

For example, asking myself, 'Jennie, what happened to you?' as I was going on a mental downward spiral, I would only get what my brain needed to hear to support my downward spiral state of mind. My brain would probably have said, 'Oh you want to know what happened to you? Well, let me TELL YOU... Jennie, this is life. You should be happy that you have a job. You are past your prime. This is normal. You are not good enough and will never be. This world is only for the favorite ones. Latinos do not succeed here. You are so naïve for having unrealistic expectations. Blah, blah, blah.'

This is exactly what happens! Do you know that your brain is doing shortcuts to "protect you" and help you feel "safe" in your comfort zone? This is why protecting, nurturing, and being very intentional with your mindset are so important.

Instead of asking a disempowering question, I asked myself these **two questions:**

- If you do nothing and choose to continue down this path (professionally and personally), will you be proud of this decision five years from now?

• What actions can you take now?

I am so glad that I asked these two questions! I'm sharing them with you because they were incredibly empowering. My answer to my first question was an absolute HECK NO! This gave me the fuel I needed to figure out next steps. I did not know the destination, but right at that moment, I knew that I needed to protect my mindset and life would show me the way. I knew I needed to prioritize myself and invest in myself.

SUCCESS IS NOT A DESTINATION

"Success is not the key to happiness. Happiness is the key to success. If you love what you are doing, you will be successful."—HERMAN CAIN

I was raised in a culture where achieving a difficult degree and a high leadership role would be translated as success. Have the best grades, be the best in class, get the highest role, and then only then, you will be successful.

Let me share a story of a friend of mine. From the time she started her career, she had a big goal of becoming a VP in the company and the industry in which she worked. She was determined to sacrifice it all, not have a family, and only focus on her career to get to the role of her dreams and her definition of success. She truly worked hard and learned everything she needed to do to be part of the "boys club," even if it was not authentic at all.

After many years of resilience, she made it! You would think she would be on top of the world, dropping the mic and relaxing for the rest of her life because she "made it" right? No, she celebrated for a hot five minutes and continued to be unsatisfied, unhappy, and now worse than anything else, regretful of her life decisions.

This was eye-opening to me because I did not want that for myself. I was also under the understanding that making it to a VP role and big site leader would have labeled me as a successful person. THIS RIGHT HERE was the BIGGEST MINDSET CHANGE that I had to navigate in my journey of starting to evaluate a career change. SUCCESS IS NOT A ROLE OR A DESTINATION.

Success is the growth journey. I changed my definition of success, and I realized that as long as I'm growing, I'm successful. I'm not talking about growing in a role or position, but growing as a person, parent, and professional. Growing in experiences, abilities, skillset, and impact!

Success is not a destination.

If you let success be a destination, you will not set yourself up for success. Let's say you work incredibly well and reach your destination. Woohoo! You made it. Then what? Once you reach it, you will start asking yourself, 'What is next?' All that work, and you celebrated for a tiny bit, and that was it. If you let the journey of growth be your success story, then you would be celebrating continuously.

Success is not a role.

If you let success be a role, you will live in a scarcity world vs. a world of abundance. For example, earlier in my career, I had in my mind one role that would "label" me as a successful professional. This goal was to be a site head of a large plant. I was so focused on this role that I did not realize that I had already been a site head. The site was a bit smaller than others, but the challenges were unique and pronounced, and that experience was incredibly rewarding.

Only focusing on one role made me feel trapped because I unconsciously narrowed my definition of success to be in one company, one area, and very few possible openings in the future. This was a very limited, stressful, and hopeless landscape.

Once I stepped back and saw the big picture, I realized that the landscape was not the little tunnel or bubble that I was in. The landscape opened up as an endless sea of opportunities, where everyone had a spot to shine!

With this new look, a successful journey could take me to many different, exciting places. Now instead of feeling trapped, I felt freedom, excitement, and joy. Hey, I don't know about you, but I would rather take the feelings of freedom, excitement, and joy over limitations, stress, and hopelessness any day!

Success is not a specific material outcome.

If you let success be a specific material outcome, you may get into the trap of comparison, not letting you enjoy the journey. Let me explain; let me share our personal journey in our house.

Ok, I should have asked my husband before writing it here. Oops! Well, I'm authentic in my sharing, and he is used to that! Jajaja (Spanish laugh). We currently live in a nice house, and what I love the most is that there is a body of water in the back that I can look at to disconnect and get a sense of calmness.

Some of our friends live in bigger houses. Also, when you see the people that talk loud about "making it," they show these humongous houses and mansions, and you tend to dream and say to yourself, 'Maybe one day.'

My husband and I even started to look for much bigger houses, with a pool, by a lake. The problem was that once you start, it is difficult to stop. We started daydreaming, thinking to ourselves, 'We will probably need a boat, a Jet-Ski, another house by the beach, and a personal plane.' Thank goodness we stopped and asked ourselves, 'Why? For external appearances? Bigger house, bigger bills, more maintenance, no thank you.'

Just to put things in perspective: If I had shown a picture of my current house to a ten-year-old version of myself, I would have said, 'WOW, JENNIE! You are going to live in a castle! Congrats on your success.'

It is always a matter of perspective. Our kids love the area, and we love our neighborhood, so we decided to make our home our dream home during the time we are here.

Don't get me wrong; I still want to retire by the beach one day. I don't care about the house; I just need to go back to the ocean. (This Puerto Rican girl is craving it!)

For now, we will invest in incredible, meaningful, and fun memories for my family by traveling and experiencing our world. It is our successful growing journey.

Another quick story about this is when people put a monetary amount as a definition of success. I have known people who have said, "When I make a million dollars, I will be successful." Then when they make it, they celebrate for a tiny bit and start comparing their journey and feel like a failure because they are not making half a billion dollars or more than a billion dollars.

You can rapidly see the vicious cycle that we can get trapped in. Instead of celebrating the successful journey, we live a life of comparison, stress, and sadness. Don't get me wrong; it is great that you put clarity on what is your next goal. Otherwise, you are driving forward with a blindfold—good luck with that. I'm referring to not letting that define you as a person or label that as your definition of success.

When it comes to money as a measure of your successful journey, you can attach it with a meaningful "WHY"? The more money I can generate, the more I can donate to the church, or help a nonprofit organization, help people in the community, or help with a big problem to solve that you connect with. Once again, this will **AMPLIFY** your successful journey.

This is my definition of success:

SUCCESS = PERSONAL GROWTH JOURNEY

PERSONAL GROWTH JOURNEY = Choices, Actions, Struggles, Learnings, Outcomes, Wins, and Impact.

Many people say that <u>"Happiness is the key to success."</u> When you hear this, you may think it means to be "happy, happy, joy, joy" at all times. However, that is not the definition of happiness. There are many definitions out there for happiness. The one that I connect with the most is the following:

HAPPINESS is an emotional state characterized by feelings of joy, satisfaction, contentment, and fulfillment.

This summarizes very well how to live an intentional and successful journey. Intentionally drive your journey with:

- <u>Joy</u>—Nurturing the right mindset, doing the things you love with the people you love.
- <u>Satisfaction</u>—Celebrating the progress and all wins, small and big.
- <u>Contentment</u>—Being grateful! Knowing that you are exactly where you need to be at this exact time. This is YOUR journey, nobody else's.
- <u>Fulfillment</u>—Attaching a personal and meaningful WHY to your goals yield very rewarding outcomes.

¿QUÉ DIRÁ LA GENTE? WHAT WOULD PEOPLE SAY?

"Care about what people think, and you will always be their prisoner."—LAO TZU

We talked about the definition of success, but what about worrying about what others would say? That was more difficult for me. Once again, I was raised in a culture where *"el que dirán"* (what would people say) was front and center, and a key consideration of every decision we made.

The reality is that WE CANNOT CONTROL what other people will say, think, or do. In fact, most of the time, we are the ones that make stories in our heads. We automatically say, "This person did this because of what I did or said." The truth is that many times we cannot be any farther than the truth.

As a fitness instructor, I used to take it very personally when people would leave in the middle of my class. I would automatically start thinking, 'They didn't like my class, why? Is my class bad? Am I not a good instructor?' My thoughts would completely ruin the rest of my class because of my personal distraction—which was not fair for the students and not good for me either.

Most of the time, the students would come back and say, "I really enjoyed your class. Too bad I could only stay for a bit because I needed to pick up a kid, or go back to work or run an errand, etc." It had NOTHING to do with me, but I let my brain run wild, focusing on something that I did not know for sure and could not control.

Several years ago, I had an employee in my organization that got promoted among their team. He started to struggle and work incredibly long hours (even above what he needed to do) to prove himself. This started to impact him and his family.

He shared with me that he was experiencing jealousy from others with a lack of welcoming behaviors, especially from a particular co-worker. He let that coworker make him feel like he was not good enough to get that promotion, and made him feel like a failure. By the way, let me insert a note here: ONLY YOU CAN MAKE YOURSELF FEEL LIKE ANYTHING; OTHER PEOPLE DON'T HAVE THAT AMOUNT OF POWER.

What he was experiencing was not matching what

everyone else was seeing. He was kicking butt in his new role with nonstop, excellent feedback from his team and customers. His supervisor and coworkers loved him.

There was one thing that he was right about: that particular coworker was not the happy person he was, and they were short and silent during this transition time. However, it had nothing to do with him. The coworker was going through a very difficult medical diagnosis. This coworker was going through a very challenging chapter of their life, and it had nothing to do with him personally. Obviously, it was not my place to share something this personal with him. I could only coach him on his great performance and focus on the things that he could control while giving everyone and himself some grace.

Here is another example: A few weeks ago, my family and I were at a restaurant. The kids love this restaurant, and we decided to go very early to make sure we did not have to wait. This particular time, we were the second family to arrive, and within minutes, the place was packed. The server took our order and then just disappeared.

Everyone around us started to get drinks, appetizers, and even food—and we had nothing. Kids started getting loud and started saying, "Not fair, everyone else is already eating, and we were one of the first ones to be there." I started to become hangry (hungry/angry). I was talking to my husband, and sharing how bad of a job our waiter was doing, that I was ready to talk to his supervisor, and I was going to give him zero tip.

My brain was already upset and making up a gazillion stories, kind of ruining our family lunch. A few minutes later, the server came to our table, apologized with very teary eyes, and shared that he just got a call and needed to leave and someone would be taking over.

I felt so bad! Here I am, only worried about our little bubble, making assumptions, and going on a spiral when in fact, it had nothing to do with us—and who knows what he was personally navigating. This was a great reminder and lesson for my family and me, to give people grace and avoid jumping to conclusions because everyone has their own story.

Last but not least, we all react to things that are very specific to our unique set of experiences, backgrounds, and perspectives. Just as I like some things and do not like others, everyone has their own preferences—and that is totally normal. All we can control is how we decide to act and react. I could not let other people's opinions (real or not) dictate the way I live and enjoy life to the fullest.

Going back to my career story, I had to learn to let go... let go of all these voices and stories in my head. Believe me, when I tell you, it was more difficult than I thought. Living according to other people's beliefs and "rules" is very ingrained in our DNAs.

I kept reminding myself of the WHY I decided to start this journey of changing careers; I kept working on believing in myself, I kept visualizing a bright future, and kept telling myself, **'Trust the process, keep moving forward with passion, you got this!'**

In Puerto Rico, we have a great slang for this: *"Pa'lante, pa'tras ni pa coger impulso,"* which means only forward, do not go back even if it is to gain momentum. Well, I think it sounds better in Spanish.

BE CONFIDENT IN WHAT YOU BRING TO THE TABLE

"Where focus goes, energy flows."—TONY ROBBINS

At this point, I was placing all my energy in prayer, training, motivational podcasts, and mentorship relationships. When you completely focus on the opportunity, it truly finds a way of finding you. One day I was at a work workshop and happened to be close to one of the company presidents during a coffee break.

The small talk turned into a conversation. "Jennie, you know I watch people..." To be honest, I did not know what to say, so I just nodded. Then he continued, "Have you ever thought of working somewhere different." I think I got so excited with the idea that my voice pitch was probably too high. I said, 'YES! I just don't know how now... it may be too late.'

He stopped me right away and recommended we

would schedule a quick lunch and talk about how that could be done. As you can imagine, I scheduled that lunch right away. We had one of the best lunches ever! He didn't offer me a job, but he gave me something better.

He reinstated the confidence in me that I needed to start this journey. We talked about what my key strengths were that were transferable into other areas. He asked what would be my ideal role, not the specific role name but the scope of the role. He shared with me a few areas to shadow and connected me with a few leaders who had something in their journey similar to mine.

One concept I learned is that you need to prioritize yourself and your goals if you want to achieve them. Otherwise, we are just relying on hope and are personifying Albert Einstein's definition of insanity: "Doing the same thing over and over and expecting a different result."

I prioritized my networking and exploratory meetings, just as if they were a priority task in my role. Was it easy? NO! I was supporting the most important product at that time in a 24/7 facility. However, I was determined, and I made it happen.

I enjoyed meeting many people. You know how that works; the more people you meet, the more you expand your network because almost everyone would recommend more people for you to know. During these meetings, I also saw that the grass isn't always greener on the other side. There were areas that would really excite me, and others that I would think, 'Thanks, but no thanks.'

A wise mentor once shared with me:

"Do not run away from something, run towards something."

This was one of the guiding principles that I used during this journey. Together with this guiding principle, I considered the following:

- Is this area a cultural fit for me?
- Will my role and outcome be meaningful?
- Will this role allow the career/life integration flexibility that I must have?
- Does the leadership in the area inspire me? Do they truly value diversity (in all of the senses of the word)?
- Is this role/area growing me as a professional?
- Will the skills learned in this role help expand my future career opportunities?
- Will this experience make me marketable?
- What would be my career progression from here?
- How much do they value what I bring to the table?

Since I am sharing like an open book (pun intended, haha), let me share my MISTAKES too! Are you ready?

- **I DISCOUNTED MY EXPERIENCE.**

- In the exploratory calls, I would start by saying, 'I know I don't have "X" experience'... Whyyyyyy? Thank goodness that I quickly learned that I needed to lead with the value that I bring and not mention what I don't have, unless they would bring it up. Of course, I was ready for that discussion; it came up in the dialog. Remember that if they have an exploratory call with you, they already know about you, and are still interested in you.

- <u>LEARNING:</u> Lead with your value!

- **I THOUGHT I NEEDED TO START FROM ZERO.**

- Even though at that time I already had ten years of experience as a senior director, I thought I needed to only look for positions at lower levels or at that level at best. During the interviews, people started to learn more about me, and started to share with me that I should be leading at a higher level! Long story short, I actually got promoted when I did the career change from the manufacturing to the business side.

  Let me add that those different areas have different perspectives on this, and there are many things in consideration (difference in role, industry, etc.). However, I want to share this to inspire you, and share that IT IS POSSIBLE! Not only did I get promoted in my company, but I also had a competing offer outside of my company for a huge promotion.

LEARNING: Be confident in your experience and expand your outlook. Be on the lookout for that next big opportunity, and go for it.

- **I GOT OVERWHELMED BY WHAT I DIDN'T KNOW.**

  - When I moved to the business area, it was like starting again in the company. New everything: areas, subjects, regulations, people, lingos, structure, etc. I went from a place where I knew so much to a place where I was learning like a rookie. That was a very humbling experience.

    However, I quickly realized that if I waited until I knew everything to provide value, that was going to be the opposite of the potential that they saw in me. My plan? I did two things in parallel:

    #1: Identified the areas where I could provide value right away based on my experience and delivered!

#2: I worked on a personal, aggressive, and intentional learning plan, working side by side with subject matter experts and inserted myself in projects that were outside of my comfort zone to learn at a faster pace.

- LEARNING: Give yourself grace, do not wait to provide value, and trust your learning agility.

- **I HESITATED AT NEGOTIATING.**

  - During my exploratory journey in my company, I got an unexpected opportunity from a competitor and a much higher level than what I was. What did I do? At first, I ignored it! I did not think I was worth that opportunity. Can you believe it?

    I casually mentioned it to my husband, and he said, "Call them!" I am so thankful that he was so insistent, because that process ended up in incredible interviews, meetings, and an amazing offer. When they asked me about what I wanted, I went for a crazy number, and they said OK! Did I feel comfortable doing this? Heck no! But my husband kept coaching me—thank goodness!

This was a very difficult decision, because the offer was so much higher than the one I had with my company. After much insistence from my husband, still with crazy emotions (pena/ pity, fear, shame, and anxiety), I shared with my potential new supervisor in my company what I was evaluating externally, and they were able to work magic and offer something that was too good to say no to. Of course, the money was not the only deciding factor, but it was great to get that feeling of being valued.

Here I was so scared of my new supervisor, thinking, "Who does she think she is?" when in fact, she reacted very positively to it. I will always remember my new supervisor's words: "I am proud of you for negotiating! You stood for your value, and this is a great sign of powerful leadership."

This whole process injected in me a sense of personal confidence that propelled a fantastic personal and career journey that continues to grow at an exponential pace.

- <u>LEARNING:</u> Speak up for your value! This is something very hard to do for many of us minority talents. Let's empower each other, educate, and close the current gap out there!

NEW CHAPTER TRANSLATED TO CONFIDENCE AND FREEDOM

"Everything that is really great and inspiring is created by the individual who can labor in freedom."
—ALBERT EINSTEIN

I went from a person that thought of herself as a board game chip/piece with no control of her next steps, to a very confident woman clear on what she is worth and what she wants out of her career.

This sense of freedom and unshakeable confidence is what I wish for you! Not only is this feeling a great one to have, but a good one to share with your family. These lessons I take with me to heart and share with my kids as I work towards being a good role model for them. They are MY WHY!

Making this career change only brought good into my life. We tend to ask, "What if it does not work?" To be proactive around this question, I did not close any doors. I kept alive my mentor relationships, continued to be visible, helping where I could (mentoring, speaking, helping some manufacturing organizations, etc.), and ensured that there was a clear alignment of my career change from both areas' senior leadership.

However, the question we should be asking instead is, "WHAT IF IT WORKS?" This question leads you to think of all the wonderful options you have to amplify and expand your career.

And there was nothing to lose! If it didn't work, I could still have opportunities to go back to manufacturing in the current or another company. If it worked, now I would have a much richer and diversified set of skills and experiences that would make me even more valuable in the future, providing more value to many more people.

Change can be terrifying. At the same time, they AMPLIFY our value! Stop and reflect on this chapter. I included a ton of learning nuggets. What resonated with you? How can you apply the learning? How can you amplify your value?

Chapter Key Takeaways:

- **SUCCESS**
  - Let's pause here and reflect! Reading books is great, but they are more powerful if you act on the learning. Otherwise, they become a decoration on the bookshelf, a donation, or a book you once listened to while you were driving and forgot what it was about.

Have in mind what you read so far in this book. Get out that journal of yours and reflect on this:

1. **What are my most important areas in life?**
   Write up to five. (Examples: faith, family, work, business, health, financial, hobbies, etc.)
2. **What is my definition of success in each area?**
3. **How can I AMPLIFY my value in each area?**

= PERSONAL GROWTH JOURNEY

Chapter 9

SHOW THE WORLD

"It's Not About Me Anymore"

This world needs the best version of you! It does not need a tired, fake, confused, or limited version. It needs your authenticity, your gifts, your experiences, your knowledge, your love, your care, your ideas, and your perspectives. The best part is that there is room for each one of us because we all bring something very different. Are you ready to show the world?

UNEXPECTED CHANGE ON MY CAREER JOURNEY

"There is no greater thing that you can do with your life and your work than follow your passions, in a way that serves the world and you."—RICHARD BRANDSON

As I was enjoying this new career in the business world, something unexpected happened. I was at a meeting that our head of DEI (Diversity, Equity, and Inclusion) put together to seek understanding and have a dialogue on how we as a company could do a better job at attracting and retaining Latinx talent. Knowing the agenda ahead of time, I did my homework and showed up ready! This is a topic that I am super passionate about, and something that I actively talk about in many external engagements and in my social media as well.

My passion for the subject was very evident to the point that the head of DEI said, "You know, the role for head of Global Talent Acquisition just opened. If you know of someone that is just as passionate as you are, let them know about this opportunity." She said this to me more as a hint.

During that meeting, I started receiving text messages from my colleagues, "Jennie, go for it! We need you there!" and I looked at all of them like they were all crazy, thinking to myself, 'Who? Me? I'm not HR!.' Once the role became public, I continued to receive calls and messages from all different people seeking my interest in the role, and I continued to ignore them all. By the time the seventh person who reached out to me, I stopped myself and thought a bit deeper about it. At this time, I was thinking, 'There is no such thing as coincidences: God, I'm hearing you now. This must be a sign.'

I truly think that I was making the term HR way more complicated than it is. I was focusing on all of the things that I did not have (HR functional experience, HR previous title, etc.). At the same time, I had a ton to bring to the role (strong cross-functional experience, many HR-related experiences, learning agility, fresh perspective, DEI passion, recruiting experience as a hiring manager and conference sponsor, and many more).

I am glad I remembered quickly from my previous career change experience to lead with my strengths and passion. Ultimately, what led me to decide to go for the role was breaking down the elements and essence of the role. Instead of thinking about HR/talent acquisition, I realized that it had a combination of two key elements and needs: DEI (my passion) and transformation (one of my superpowers!).

There were many incredible leaders going after this role. I could have easily gotten distracted by comparing myself with the others, but instead, I did something simple. Don't laugh, but this is what I did: I drew a heart on an orange sticky note and inside of the heart I wrote: 'Passion and opportunity to impact many.' I placed this sticky note on my computer monitor, and this was my focus and intention throughout all of the interviews.

In addition to preparing for the interview, I focused on three things: what I could control; sharing examples of the leader I am and the impact I would have on the organization and company; I brought authenticity and confidence. Now it was up to them. If I was the leader they needed, they would offer me the role—and they DID!

In the past, I would say that I had a career, and on the side, I was doing the things that I was passionate about. Now I got to the point where all things in my life aligned in a magical manner. When that happens, that's when you amplify your value and share it with the world!

MY PANDEMIC BABY

"Don't be afraid to fail. Be afraid not to try."
—MICHAEL JORDAN

The pandemic years were years of deep reflection for many of us. Many things ended, pivoted, or started as a result of such a historical moment like that one. I was one of the people who had a pandemic baby—not an actual baby, not a puppy, but a business!

Having gone through the journey of two very different career changes in a successful manner gave me the confidence and realization that I could tackle anything I would dream of. I had a good combination of experience, learning agility, resilience, and passion for getting me moving to the next chapter of my life.

I decided to invest heavily in myself and on how to continue to grow to be the best version of me in this journey called LIFE. I read tons of books, I listened to numerous podcasts, and I experienced many immersion education and training programs that would cover everything from limiting beliefs, mindset, vision, business, strategies, and many more. During this time, I realized that **I was placed in this world at this exact time for a reason.**

I reflected on these three points, and I am sharing them with you so you can also reflect on them:

<u>My personal vision:</u>
- What is the problem that you want to solve?
- When you connect the dots of your life, how do they amplify your vision? (e.g., learnings, experiences, achievements)

<u>My WHY:</u>
- Why is this worth it? Why does this matter?
- Who will benefit from it? How will they benefit from it?

My next steps:
- Where are you now? Where do you want to go?
- What is your plan? What is your best next step?

MY PERSONAL VISION

What I love to do the most is coaching, mentoring, and helping others get to the next big step in their journey. This is the main reason I decided to pursue management in my career.

Looking back at my career, I was happy with my achievements. At the same time, I know in my heart that it should not have to be ten times harder for minority talent to get to their goals as it is for their majority counterparts. For me, this was my a-ha moment!

Can I leverage my experiences, my authenticity, my energy, and passion to do anything from my end to help close that gap in representation? And this is how my pandemic baby was born!

MY WHY

Once you have a dream, the best thing you can do is to attach a super strong and powerful WHY to it. This WHY is what will help you and give you the fuel and momentum you need to keep pushing forward, especially when challenges and obstacles arise.

We talked about this earlier in the book. This is how you can get to a much deeper why. This is an exercise that you can do at any time.

Ask yourself why your dream is important and why now. Then don't stop at the first answer; ask yourself again, WHY? Just as toddlers keep asking "WHY?, WHY?, WHY?" just like that. Stop when you get to your #5 or #7 level deep WHY. You will know when you get there, because your whole body will resonate, and tears may even roll down because of the depth and personal realization.

Do you want to know my personal WHY? My kids! I don't want them to have to go through what I did to have a successful career or business. I want to raise them with very strong confidence in themselves. I want all of us to be the change agents that we need to create a world where everyone can shine bright with their unique gifts in total freedom.

MY NEXT STEPS

I knew what I wanted and why. I also knew that I needed to take massive action if I was all in towards making my vision a reality.

Two things were very key here:

1. **I took massive action:** This was when I had to close a chapter in my life. For the past seven years, I had been working as an education specialist (master trainer) for a very well-known global fitness company. As much as I loved it, it

was taking a ton of my time (the most valuable resource). I also was at a point where my growth in the role had reached a level where I was very happy, but not personally challenged. I was also sharing somebody else's message, and now it was time for me to spread my wings and focus on an area that is very much needed and not many people are focusing on.

I am forever grateful for that chapter because of the incredible experiences and all the people I impacted by teaching them fitness. The teaching and presenting experience also gave me a very solid foundation for my next chapter as a professional speaker and coach.

I also decided to go all in towards investing in myself... not later "when I had time, when I feel like it, when it is convenient"... **AT THAT EXACT TIME!** "Tomorrow" was not guaranteed, and this need is urgent.

The best time to start is NOW, not yesterday (it is gone), not tomorrow (not here yet). Now, your turn, what is that massive action that you must take NOW?

2. **I ensured I had a strong accountability system:** When it comes to accountability, I am lucky to count on my husband. He also decided to join me

in many of these education immersion programs, which was fantastic because he started to work on his own journey. We also started to talk the same 'lingo' and started holding each other accountable, and even coached each other when we saw each other going back to previous behaviors or beliefs. I also invested in a business coach, who has been an incredible partner and key pillar through my journey in creating my business and making my vision a reality.

Last but not least, I committed to bold goals and surrounded myself with people and mentors that cheered on me and held me accountable as well. What resources do you have to ensure that you have a strong accountability system in your journey?

MEET BRUNA.... MY IMPOSTOR SYNDROME

"Doubt will kill more dreams than failure ever will."
—SUZY KASSEM

Almost every time someone reads my bio and introduces me before I go on stage, I experience this crazy feeling and ask myself, 'Who are they talking about? Wow, they are pretty cool! Who is this person?' It is like they are talking about someone very accomplished, but that person is not me.

In my head, I am still a very young girl that not everyone takes seriously or believes in, because she is still not good enough for their standards. Do you ever feel like this? It is an out-of-body experience.

Impostor Syndrome basically describes the feeling when you doubt your abilities and feel like you are a fraud. I first heard of the term 'Impostor Syndrome' in 2017, even though it was first "identified" in the 1970s. Back then, it was theorized that women were uniquely affected by it. In reality, everyone feels this several times in their lives. The frequency and the magnitude depend on the person and their experiences. I can speak for females and minority talent, where this feeling is amplified because of our cultural upbringing and society norms.

Since we know that all of us (even the most famous people) go through this, the key is how to recognize when this is happening and right away stop it and say "NOT TODAY."

You can even have fun with it and name it. For example, the name of my nagging', nay-sayer, doubter, annoying *vocecita en mi cabeza* (little voice in my head) is BRUNA. I got inspired by the movie LUCA.

Not sure if you have seen the movie LUCA, but it is a very cute animated film that takes place in Italy. The main character is Luca, and his best friend is trying to teach him a challenging bike ride, while trying different models of bikes.

Luca was scared, and he tells his best friend, "I can't do it." His best friend then says, "You have BRUNO in your head. You just have to say *Silenzio*, (Silence) Bruno." Luca kept repeating those words even when he was still scared, *"Silenzio Bruno, Silenzio Bruno, Silenzio Bruno,"* until he got the confidence to go for it. Ultimately, they got very good at it and successfully competed in a race in their town.

This was a beautiful way to demonstrate that there is a bright adventure and future when you overcome your limiting beliefs. So now, have fun with it and name your Impostor Syndrome. What name did you come up with? Remember when they get loud (your impostor), get the confidence to tell them, "NOT TODAY!"

BUILDING THE CONFIDENCE MUSCLE

"Your success will be determined by your own confidence and fortitude."—MICHELLE OBAMA

I started my business with excitement and a hot five seconds later, I got paralyzed with FEAR! This fear came fast and furious, sustained by my own personal limiting beliefs and BRUNA (Impostor Syndrome).

I remember sharing this with my coach, and she smiled and shared that this was totally normal, and it actually happens to every entrepreneur. She shared with me the concept of the **CHAIR**, and I want to share it with you as well.

The fear that I had was based on my beliefs. I had two main personal limiting beliefs: I was not good enough (did not have enough credentials) for what I wanted to achieve, and my family and the people I knew were going to laugh at me. I thought they were going to think that I was greedy, because I already had a good career; why did I want to do more?

Here is where the concept of the CHAIR comes in handy. Your **personal belief** is the **'seat'** of the chair. For the seat to be stable, it needs to stand on solid legs. The **'legs'** of the chair are **evidence and facts** that sustain the belief.

Let's take my beliefs as examples; did they hold on to steady legs?

- <u>"I am not enough. I have no credentials."</u>—**False**! Yes, I was prepared! In reality, I have had years of experience teaching and speaking in both my engineering career and fitness/dance career. In addition, I was even awarded for my teaching and coaching skills. I had learned a ton from my career and this is the learning that I wanted to share with the world. This knowledge needed to be shared, so we could help accelerate talent and change the status quo. In addition to the learnings, I have had a great career journey and have gotten to a place of influence and even considered a thought leader in my space. Conclusion: The legs do not sustain the seat!

- "People will laugh. People will think I'm greedy."– **False!** First of all, I had not even shared it with my parents or friends, and when I did, everyone was extremely supportive. Second, I do have many stories where I have helped many people get to their goals and really change their lives. And last but not least, when I share my vision, I get the same reaction, "This is so needed. Thank you for what you do!" Conclusion: These thoughts were all in my head, with no facts or supporting legs for the seat.

Once you realize that your limiting beliefs have no supporting legs, then you change the chair seat to an **EMPOWERING BELIEF.** My empowering belief changed to be "I am an impactful leader." Did that seat have strong legs? YES!!! Many of them.

Do this exercise with those limiting beliefs that you have! Go to a place where you can concentrate and journal all your thoughts. I promise that you will start building that confidence muscle that you must have to pursue those meaningful goals that you have.

Two bonus points regarding building confidence. This should be more of a reminder, since we have covered these concepts, but repetition is what makes skill stick and evolve.

- **Do not compare your journey to others.** Your journey is unique in all the senses of the word (It's YOU! Your story, approach, experience, vision, connection, pace, timing). Comparing your journey to anyone else's is not an apples to apples comparison, and it will not serve you well. Focus on your own journey and on becoming a better version of what you were yesterday. People connect with authenticity, not carbon copies. When you are authentic to your journey, you can evolve and share your best you with the world!
- **Focus on what you can control.** Will there be people that make fun of me? Will there be doubters? Will there be people who think that I'm greedy? I am sure there are. Can I control them? No, however, that's on them, not on me.

Will there be people out there that will benefit from what I have to say? Yes! Will I have the same life-changing impact that I experienced on others? Yes, I will. They are the people I want to help. They are my focus. What I can control is my actions, my focus on how I can positively impact the most people I can, and the personal discipline I must have to not give up, stay energized and make my vision a reality.

A big watch out is how our culture and upbringing can wire limiting beliefs in our brain. These wired limiting beliefs can play a huge role in our beliefs, decisions, actions, and approaches. Why? Because they were said to us so many times that they got programmed into our subconscious minds.

Let me go over this definition here very quickly and at a super high level. **The conscious mind** involves rationalizing and logical thinking. **The subconscious mind** pretty much takes everything literal and is responsible for involuntary actions.

For example, in Latino/Latina/Latinx/Hispanic culture, we have several idioms, slang, proverbs, and sayings that were repeated to us time and time again. Here are a few of disempowering and limiting ones:

IDIOM / SLANG	MEANING
"Calladita más bonita"	You look better when you are quiet.
"Ya te casaste, ya se acabaron tus sueños"	You just got married, your dreams are over.
"El dinero no crece en árboles"	Money does not grow on trees

"Tienes que trabajar doble para que vean tu valor"	You have to do double the work for others to see your value.
"Árbol que crece torcido jamás su tronco endereza"	A tree that grows crooked never gets straightened out.
"Mas vale pájaro en mano que 100 volando"	Better to have a bird on your hand than see 100 flying. Meaning to be contempt with what is secure and safe than going for the unknown.
"Para lucir hay que sufrir"	You have to suffer to be able to look good.
"Eso es de hombres"	That's for men.
"El dinero es sucio"	Money is dirty.
"Tienes que tener un hijo para ser una mujer completa"	You have to have a child to be a complete woman.
"No por mucho madrugar amanece más temprano"	Even when you wake up earlier, the day will always start at the same time. In other words, time will always take its course.

The danger here is when we say them, we believe in them as they are a matter of fact.

I remember one time talking to the parent of one of my students at a kids fitness class, and he was sharing with me everything that was going wrong with his job, the toxic culture, the crazy long hours that he was working, and the fact that he did not have time to spend with the kids.

Before I was able to say anything, he told me, *"Bueno, pero así es la vida... pero mas vale pájaro en mano que 100 volando,"* and then he left right away. I was shocked at how he was just seeing that this was his life, and he had no other options to have more time with his family or even generate more income.

This is where we need to act quickly. Acknowledge what you say or think, then ask yourself, 'Is this true?' Once you realize this is a limiting belief with NO LEGS, then you transform it into a new EMPOWERING one.

Try it. Journal now three to five disempowering beliefs that you have and transform them into empowering beliefs! When you catch yourself saying or thinking the old disempowering belief, correct yourself with the new empowering one!

WORKING ON AUTHENTIC CONFIDENCE

"Authenticity is when you say and do the things you actually believe."—SIMON SINEK

What is authenticity? **Authenticity** is being genuine, being exactly what is claimed, and being trustworthy. If you also look for the meaning of **confidence**, you will also see descriptions like trustworthiness, reliability, and assurance. The way to get to the goals that you are striving for is by working and growing your authentic confidence.

Authentic confidence is honest, well-intentioned, and focused on serving. **Authentic confidence is not** arrogant, selfish, and ego-centered.

Some people forgo being confident because they do not want to be seen as "that person" that embodies those characteristics that are not centered on authentic confidence. They are avoiding to be the know it all, fake, all for themselves, egotistic, and the conceited person they have experienced in the past.

Other people shy away from being confident because they say things like "I'm shy," "I'm introverted," or "I do not know it all." They have internalized these labels, and in their minds, such as there is no other way, and this is who they are.

But what if I tell you that everyone in this world can be authentically confident? First, the authenticity part you own! That's the easy part if you are intentional with it. There is only ONE YOU! Second, the confidence part you work on it just like going to the gym; you keep working at it.

By now, you probably know me a bit more. The go-getter, the person who loves to perform, dance, and speak to many audiences. If you see me on social media, you see the energetic, crazy lady that one day can be all dolled up in a pretty dress and the next day in PJs dancing without makeup or hair done, but still sharing a positive message.

Would you believe me if I told you that I was a very shy girl growing up? My parents would be worried because I would not make friends at birthday parties. However, my parents pushed me to do things, to be the one to ask strangers for things, to participate in school shows and activities, etc.

When I first started my career, I was terrified of giving presentations in front of people. What did I do? I worked and worked on it a ton. I'm still working on it, and I still do not believe it, but I am now a professional speaker. And yet, I still get asked to do some big events, and my mind first goes to the fearful place, but quickly, I say yes and commit. These are the experiences that continue to grow my confidence muscle.

Confidence is up for grabs for all of us. I have even seen it in my fitness dance classes. It goes like this: the student says, "I'm new, please don't mind me, I'll be in the back." They keep coming to class and slowly move one row at a time from the back of the room to the first row. The next thing you see is that they are on stage dancing next to me.

I have seen this with students of ALL AGES! It is the most wonderful experience as a teacher to see the change in their entire physiology, gaining the most important life skill there is to have. Confidence impacts your happiness, well-being, and success.

Here are a few strategies that you can do to take confidence to the gym:

- **Remember a previous win.** Think back of a time when you were able to achieve something great, or able to navigate through a very difficult situation, or figure out a life-changing problem. All of us have at least one of those incredible moments. One of those moments that you probably told yourself once, "There is no way..." But you did it! How did you do it? How did you feel? This now should give you the confidence that if you did that once... you can do it again and again! All you need is inside of you.

- **Do something new!** Nothing like putting yourself in a new situation with a beginner's mind. Nobody, not even yourself, is expecting to be an expert from day one, quite the opposite. With persistence and consistency, you will see yourself grow in this new area, and the confidence that comes with this is priceless!

- **Prepare.** For anything in life where you want to grow, make sure you are intentional in your preparation and do not go on autopilot. Even in your current role—what are you doing to ensure you continue to grow instead of going day by day according to your meeting schedule and your to do list?

Things to think about: Are you preparing before the meeting, so you have a visible key role the next day? Are you networking? Are you asking for challenging projects/assignments that will make you grow? Are you looking for growth opportunities outside of your job (church, school, advisory councils, boards, etc.)? Are you learning a skill that will be needed in the future in your field? Are you mastering your strengths? Are keeping up with external trends?

- **Change the definition of FAILURE.** We talked about this previously in this book, and here we are again, because it is that important. The FEAR of FAILURE is what stops us from going after something great. Let's do something... let's eliminate that word from our vocabulary. We are calling it LEARNING. Learning means that you try something, you learn, you grow, and you repeat. Learning is necessary for everything we are striving to do.

  Give it a try. Do something (you can start with something small) that you have been thinking about doing but are scared that it may not work. Perhaps you are scared of other people's responses (let's remember we cannot control that). Now, GO FOR IT... learn... grow. You will never see what is on the other side if you just stop now. Let's learn and grow!

IT IS NOT ABOUT ME ANYMORE

"Do not wait for leaders; do it alone, person to person. Be faithful in small things because it is in them that your strength lies."—MOTHER TERESA

CLARITY is key. Once I got the clarity on what my personal mission was, I was determined to take this exciting journey and grow with it. See how I did not use words like nerve-racking, uncertain, unknown, and terrifying? **The power words have in our lives and approaches is stunning.** Watch out for your words and use them to your advantage and momentum!

This is when the next phase of your life journey is to SHARE IT WITH THE WORLD. Whatever that is for you. You need clarity on a rewarding career, the memories you want to create for your family, the places you want to visit, the well-being level you want to achieve, the area where you want to volunteer, the business you want to create, the impact you want to have in your community, the legacy you want to leave in this world.

Now that you are working towards growing your authentic confidence, think about not only the impact this journey has on you, but the impact you will have on others. When you switch your focus from you only to serving others, this is when you start growing at a much higher pace. Your focus on helping others will give you the gift of inspiration, innovation, and resilience.

Remember that you do not have to do it alone. In fact, we should be surrounding ourselves all the time with people that will make us better people, that will cheer for us, will empower us, and will teach us in one way or another.

Many of us feel like talking about ourselves or about our goals and dreams may be perceived as egotistic or conceited. However, we need to change this belief, because otherwise, we will continue to be invisible, and this will stop us from helping others at our best. Neither you nor I want to be the best secret in this world. Instead, you need to voice and communicate your value, experience, and goals this way you can work towards moving to the points where you can help and serve more people, amplifying your value.

Amplifying your value and sharing it with the world requires intentionality. It requires putting yourself in not-so-comfortable situations so you can continue to expand your circle of influence and expand your reality. Remember that NEW = GROWTH.

Just as we learned in the last chapter, you want to continue to expand your reality. Think of the drawing where your initial world/reality was a little box, but every time you step out of your comfort zone, you get into a bigger box amplifying your world/reality.

This process can also be a bit exhausting if you go, go, go, and don't pause to reflect and recharge! Here are a few tips on how you can do this:

- Fill your cup
- Start/end your day in appreciation and gratitude
- Add reflection days to your calendar (aka no meetings, only reflection and strategic work)
- Every week, ask yourself "What are we celebrating?" (Acknowledge every win—small or big!)
- Prioritize your well-being
- Simply take time off to recharge!

In this growing journey, there is no final destination. I have heard the saying: "If you are not growing, you are dying." It may sound a bit morbid, but think about it; nothing good comes from anything that is stagnant.

If you let me be a bit nerdy here, let's talk about Newton's law of motion: "An object will not change its motion unless a force acts on it." What is this force for you? This can come in many ways... going for a promotion, adding education, expanding your network, becoming a social media influencer, creating your own opportunities, starting a podcast, changing careers, helping the community, teaching others, writing a book, creating a group, and sharing your story just to mention a few. SHOW THE WORLD!

YES, I AM A UNICORN, AN INTENTIONAL ONE

"Be heard, be seen, and be felt."—JENNIE LOPEZ—ME!

Do I still feel like I stand out with my horn? Absolutely! However, I am now proud of it, and empower others to do the same! I live my life intentionally to continue to grow and have as much impact as I can. Do I know what the future holds for me? No, but that is the beauty of it and how we make this wonderful chapter called LIFE a beautiful and meaningful one.

You, too, can and will get to that next goal and dream of yours. In this book, I shared the spiral concept that will help you thrive in life.

- DECIDE
- COMMIT
- TAKE ACTION
- ADAPT
- INVEST
- CREATE
- AMPLIFY
- SHOW THE WORLD

At the beginning of the book, I showed you a very pretty spiral with a beginning and end. Nonetheless, life is not a straight line; neither is it a pretty, fixed spiral. It will take you on crazy turns and unexpected events but they are part of your own growing journeys. You heard me right: grow in spirals, because you will continue to grow it and maximize it.

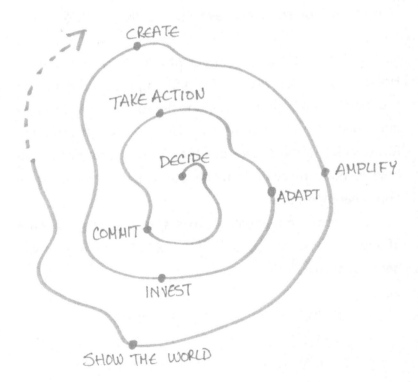

We need more role models! Be someone that is helping create a culture where everyone embraces all of our superpowers, uniqueness to best serve others, and leave a powerful legacy for the next generation to continue to enhance.

All of us are unicorns. We came to this world to live up to our uniqueness and live a meaningful life in our own ways. Imagine if all of us UNICORNS knew exactly what we bring and used it intentionally to make life impactful and rewarding lives for ourselves, the people we love, and the world we live in.

The biggest lesson of all was knowing exactly who I AM, owning my unicorn profile, and building confidence in what I bring (my superpowers), so I can have an impact on the world that I want to help shape.

This is exactly what I want for you: WHO ARE YOU? How are you going to apply the lessons learned to help you drive your own authentic, successful journey?

Remember to bring your own CONFIDENT and AUTHENTIC UNICORN into every aspect of your life.

Be heard.
Be seen.
Be felt.
BE YOU!

ABOUT THE AUTHOR

When you imagine a woman who is not only a corporate powerhouse but brings that same intensity, energy, and talent to everything she touches, Jennie Lopez should be the first person you think of.

She is a woman of contrasts. A chemical engineer. A professional dancer. A fitness instructor. An author. A wife and mom. A board member. Even more, Jennie is an "Avatar" for success. Whenever she sets a goal, this Puerto Rico native makes the magic happen and has another achievement to be proud of.

Some people talk about authenticity, and others live it. Jennie doesn't have to tell you that being authentic is vital to her outlook. She lives life as an intentional unicorn, bringing authenticity and magic by intention to everything she does.

It has become so much a part of her that Jennie authored a book titled Intentional Unicorn. She has discovered that there is power in UNIqueness that fuels confidence and allows her to embrace everything she is.

Rather than fitting in, Jennie intentionally stands out, much like a unicorn does. She used her Latinx heritage, passions, life lessons, and experience as a mom to build the strength she needed to find personal and professional success. Now she helps others do the same and find their inner unicorn, too.

Along her professional path, Jennie moved to the U.S. to complete her master's degree in chemical engineering. This led to leadership roles in manufacturing and quality and later took her to the business side as a global brand leader, senior leader, and chief operating officer. She is currently the Associate VP of Global Talent Acquisition for a pharmaceutical company.

Jennie is also an executive board member for the Organization of Latinx, focusing on developing and accelerating Latinx talent, and in 2021 joined the board of directors for Genesis Research. No matter where she is, Jennie often takes the lead to empower diversity and challenge employees and organizations to achieve new highs.

Her success doesn't stop there. Jennie has also found great success in dancing and fitness. Her vast number of experiences include time as a professional dancer for artists like Julio Iglesias and Ednita Nazario, TV shows, NFL cheerleader and captain for a Superbowl-winning team, national fitness instructor, presenter, and Zumba master trainer.

As a well-known business owner, speaker, and author, Jennie wrote Intentional Unicorn, is a contributing author for Hispanic Stars Rising, Vol. 2, and is frequently invited to be a guest speaker for many local and national organizations.

Jennie's accomplishments also spill over to the personal side, where she was presented with the 2020 Working Mother of the Year award. She enjoys making intentional fun memories with her husband, Brad, and her children, Izzie (11) and Ethan (8). They are the WHY behind everything she does.